SIXTH EDITION
GRAMMAR IN CONTEXT BASIC

SANDRA N. ELBAUM
JUDI P. PEMÁN

NATIONAL GEOGRAPHIC LEARNING | CENGAGE Learning

Australia • Brazil • Mexico • Singapore • United Kingdom • United States

Contents **v**

A word from the authors **ix**

contextualized clear examples
of the structure.

Welcome to *Grammar in Context* **xi**

I am grateful to the team at National Geographic Learning/Cengage Learning for showing

Welcome to **GRAMMAR IN CONTEXT,** Sixth Edition

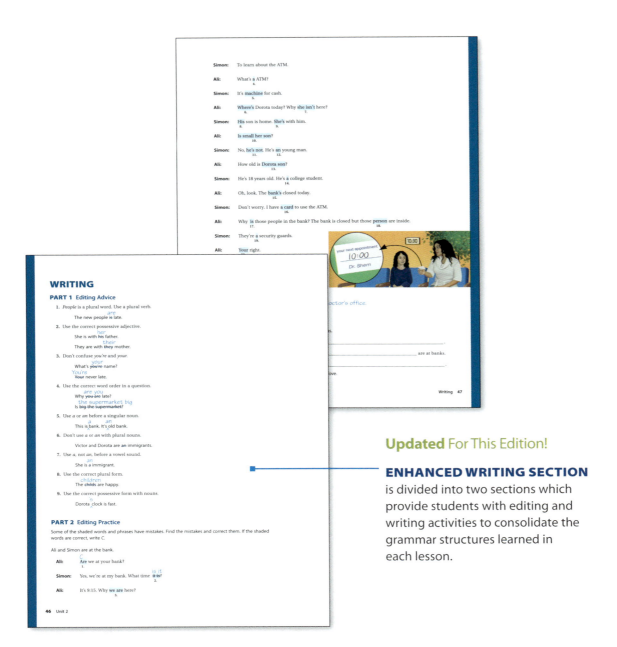

Updated For This Edition!

ENHANCED WRITING SECTION
is divided into two sections which
provide students with editing and
writing activities to consolidate the
grammar structures learned in
each lesson.

ADDITIONAL RESOURCES FOR EACH LEVEL

Updated For This Edition!

ONLINE WORKBOOK

powered by MyELT provides students with additional practice of the target grammar and greater flexibility for independent study.

- Engages students and supports classroom materials by providing a variety of interactive grammar activities.

- Tracks course completion through student progress bars, giving learners a sense of personal achievement.

- Supports instructors by maximizing valuable learning time through course management resources, including scheduling and grade reporting tools.

Go to NGL.Cengage.com/MyELT

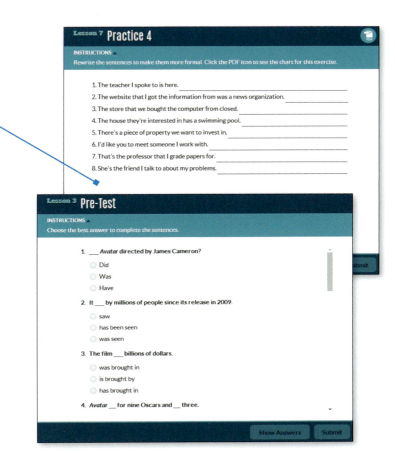

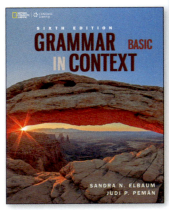
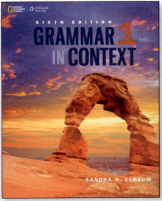
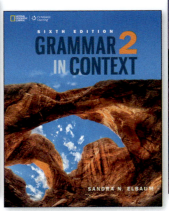
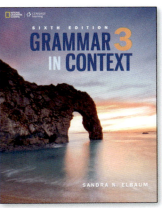

Simon and Marta, with Tina, Amy, and Ed

Halina and Peter, with Anna

Dorota

Shafia and Ali

Victor and Lisa, with Maya

Sue and Rick

View of New York Harbor from
the top of the Statue of Liberty

Welcome TO THE UNITED STATES

Here is not merely a nation but a teeming nation of nations.

— Walt Whitman

1

GRAMMAR
Subject Pronouns
Be—Affirmative Statements

CONTEXT
Help for New Immigrants

An exhibit at the Immigration Museum on Ellis Island, New York, NY

BEFORE YOU READ

Circle *yes* or *no*.

1. Many things are new for me in this country.   Yes   No

2. People help me with new things.   Yes   No

READ

CD 1
TR 2

Read the following conversation. Pay special attention to the subject pronouns and *is, am,* and *are* in bold.

Dorota and Simon are at the airport.

Dorota: Welcome! My name **is** Dorota. **I am** from Poland, but **I am** a citizen of the U.S.[1] now. My first language **is** Polish. English **is** my second language. This **is** my friend, Simon. **He is** from Mexico.

Simon: Hi. My name **is** Simon. **I am** from Mexico, but **I am** a citizen of the U.S. now too. Spanish **is** my first language. My second language **is** English. **We are** both here to help you. **We are** helpful.

Dorota: **You are** new in this country. **You are** immigrants from other countries. Life **is** different here. Many things **are** different for you—the supermarket **is** different, the laundromat **is** different, and the bank and school **are** different too. Everything **is** new for you. Maybe **you are** confused.

Simon: Dorota and **I are** here to help you in new places. The laundromat and supermarket **are** the first places to go.

_____

[1] *U.S.* is an abbreviation for United States.

DID YOU KNOW?
Some supermarkets and laundromats are open 24 hours a day.

Vocabulary	Context
citizen	Dorota is a **citizen** of the United States.
first/second	The **first** place to go is the laundromat. The next place is the supermarket. The supermarket is **second**.
both	Dorota is a citizen. Simon is too. They are **both** citizens.
help (v.) helpful (adj.)	Dorota and Simon **help** new immigrants. They are **helpful**.
immigrant	I am from Colombia. I am new to the United States. I am an **immigrant**.
life	**Life** in the United States is new for me.
different	Simon is from Mexico. Dorota is from Poland. They are from **different** countries.
supermarket	We buy food in a **supermarket**.
laundromat	The **laundromat** is a place to wash clothes.
bank	He needs money. He is at the **bank**.
everything	**Everything** is new—the bank, the supermarket, and the laundromat.
confused	I am new here. Everything is different. I am **confused**.

2

GRAMMAR

Contractions (Short Forms)

Singular and Plural

This, That, These, Those

CONTEXT

Using the Laundromat

This Illinois laundromat has 145 washers and 125 dryers and runs on solar power.

BEFORE YOU READ

Circle *yes* or *no*.

1. I use the laundromat.   Yes   No

2. I wash my clothes by hand.   Yes   No

READ

Read the following conversation. Pay special attention to contractions with *be* and *this, that, these* and *those* in bold.

Dorota and a new immigrant, Shafia, are at the laundromat.

Dorota: **This** is the laundromat.

Shafia: The **laundromat's** new for me. **I'm** a little confused.

Dorota: Don't worry. **We're** together. **I'm** here to help you.

Shafia: Thanks. My clothes are dirty. I need clean clothes. **I'm** glad **we're** here.

Dorota: **These** are the washing machines, or washers. The small machines are for small items—clothes, towels, and sheets. **Those** big machines are for big items, like blankets. Coins are necessary for the machines. Over there is the change machine.

Shafia: **Those** machines over there are different.

Dorota: Yes. **They're** dryers. They are for the wet clothes.

Shafia: Okay. Wow! **It's** hot inside the laundromat.

Dorota: **You're** right. The dryers are very hot.

Shafia: **It's** easy to wash clothes in a laundromat.

Dorota: Yes, it is.

Shafia: **These** two washers are empty. **I'm** ready to wash my clothes.

DID YOU **KNOW?**

The average American family washes almost 400 loads of laundry each year.

Vocabulary	Context
don't worry	**Don't worry.** I'm here to help you.
together	Dorota is with Shafia. They're **together**.
clothes	This is my shirt. Those are my pants. These are my **clothes**.
dirty	Your clothes are **dirty**. You need to wash them.
clean	My clothes are **clean**. I don't need to wash mine.
glad	I'm **glad** we're here. I'm happy.
item	These machines are for small **items**. Those machines are for bigger things.
necessary	It's **necessary** to wash clothes. You need to do it.
change machine	When you put a dollar bill in the **change machine** it gives you coins. Four quarters is **change** for one dollar.
right	**A:** It's hot here. **B:** Yes, you're **right**. It is hot.
empty	The dryer is **empty**. It is available.
ready	**A:** It's time to go. **B:** Yes, I'm **ready**! We can go.

LISTEN

CD 1
TR 6

Listen to the sentences about the conversation. Circle *true* or *false*.

1. (True)   False   4. True   False

2. True   False   5. True   False

3. True   False   6. True   False

1.3 Contractions (Short Forms)

Long Form	Contraction	Examples
I am	I'm	**I'm** here to help.
She is	She's	**She's** from Poland.
He is	He's	**He's** from Mexico.
It is	It's	**It's** hot in here.
Life is	Life's	**Life's** different.
Everything is	Everything's	**Everything's** new.
Dorota is	Dorota's	**Dorota's** from Poland.
The laundromat is	The laundromat's	The **laundromat's** hot.
You are	You're	**You're** very helpful.
We are	We're	**We're** together.
They are	They're	**They're** at the laundromat.

Language Notes:

1. To make a contraction (short form), we put an apostrophe (') in place of the missing letter.

2. We can make a contraction with a subject pronoun + *am, is,* and *are.*

3. We can make a contraction with a singular subject + *is.*

4. We cannot make a contraction with a plural noun + *are.*

    The **dryers are** empty.   NOT: The **dryers're** empty.

Kolkata, India

EXERCISE 1 Write the contraction for the words given.

1. _____I'm_____ new here.
   <small>I am</small>

2. _____ from Mexico.   _____ a citizen of the United States now.
   <small>a. Simon is</small>   <small>b. He is</small>

3. _____ from Poland.   _____ a citizen too.
   <small>a. Dorota is</small>   <small>b. She is</small>

4. _____ both very helpful.
   <small>They are</small>

5. _____ big.
   <small>The laundromat is</small>

6. _____ hot in the laundromat.
   <small>It is</small>

7. _____ new here.   _____ new too.   _____ both new.
   <small>a. You are</small>   <small>b. I am</small>   <small>c. We are</small>

EXERCISE 2 Ali and Peter are new immigrants. This is their conversation. Fill in the blanks with the
<small>CD 1 TR 7</small> correct form of *be*. Use contractions when possible.

Ali: I <u>'m</u> from India. You <u>'re</u> from Russia, right?
<small>1.</small>   <small>2.</small>

Peter: No. I _____ from Warsaw. It _____ in Poland.
<small>3.</small>   <small>4.</small>

Ali: I _____ new here. I _____ confused about things.
<small>5.</small>   <small>6.</small>

Peter: We _____ both confused. Life _____ different here.
<small>7.</small>   <small>8.</small>

Ali: Yes. Many things _____ new here. The bank _____ new for me.
<small>9.</small>   <small>10.</small>

The supermarket _____ new for me too.
<small>11.</small>

Peter: I _____ glad to know Simon and Dorota. Simon and Dorota _____ from other countries,
<small>12.</small>   <small>13.</small>

but they _____ both citizens now. Simon _____ from Mexico. He _____ helpful.
<small>14.</small>   <small>15.</small>   <small>16.</small>

Dorota _____ from Poland. She _____ helpful too.
<small>17.</small>   <small>18.</small>

Ali: You _____ right. They _____ both very helpful to new immigrants.
<small>19.</small>   <small>20.</small>

Warsaw Castle Square, Poland

1.4 Singular and Plural

Singular means one. *Plural* means more than one. A plural noun usually ends in *-s*.

Singular	Plural	Singular	Plural
one machine	five machine**s**	one laundromat	four laundromat**s**
one coin	six coin**s**	one supermarket	seven supermarket**s**
one towel	three towel**s**	one friend	nine friend**s**
one blanket	two blanket**s**	one citizen	eight citizen**s**

EXERCISE 3 Write the plural form of the words.

quarter

dime

nickel

dollar

1. sheet   *sheets*

2. quarter   _____

3. dime   _____

4. dryer   _____

5. nickel   _____

6. machine   _____

7. towel   _____

8. item   _____

9. blanket   _____

10. coin   _____

11. dollar   _____

12. citizen   _____

1.5 *This, That, These, Those*

Singular	Plural	Explanation
This is a laundromat.	**These** are quarters.	Near →
That is a big machine.	**Those** are the dryers.	Not near Far →

Language Note:

Only *that is* has a contraction—*that's*.

   That's a big machine.

Pronunciation Note:

It's hard for many nonnative speakers to hear the difference between *this* and *these*. Listen to your teacher pronounce the sentences in the chart.

EXERCISE 4 Fill in the blanks with *this, that, these,* or *those* and the correct form of *be*. Use contractions when possible.

1.  _____This is_____ a dollar.

2.  _____ the change machine.

3.  _____ coins.

4.  _____ quarters.

5.  _____ the big washing machines.

6.  _____ an empty machine.

7. _____ dryers.

EXERCISE 5 Circle the correct word.

1. The (*sheet /* *sheets*) are white.

2. The blankets (*is / are*) big.

3. (*These / This*) are the dryers.

4. (*They're / They*) hot.

5. (*A quarter / Quarters*) are necessary for the machine.

6. (*That / Those*) machines are empty.

3

CONTEXT

At the Supermarket

A woman looks at vegetables in a supermarket.

BEFORE YOU READ

Circle *yes* or *no*.

1. I'm confused in an American supermarket.   Yes   No

2. Prices are the same in every supermarket.   Yes   No

READ

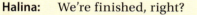

Read the following conversation. Pay special attention to negative forms of *be*, adjectives, and expressions with *It* in bold.

Dorota and Halina are at the supermarket.

Dorota: This is the supermarket. **It's early.** The supermarket **isn't crowded**. The parking lot's **not crowded**.

Halina: This is my first time in an American supermarket. I**'m not** sure what to do.

Dorota: **It's not hard** to use the supermarket. I'm here to help you.

Halina: Thanks. Hmmm. The prices **aren't** on the products.

Dorota: The prices are on the shelves, under the products. A bar code is on each package. Prices **aren't** the same every week. Some things are on sale each week. Look—crackers are on sale this week. They're usually $3.99 a box. This week they**'re not** $3.99 a box. They're $2.50. And look there. Apples are on sale too. One pound for $1.15.

Halina: Look! These cookies are **free**.

Dorota: The samples are **free**, but the bags of cookies **aren't**.

(ten minutes later)

Halina: We're finished, right?

Dorota: Yes, we're finished. This checkout is **empty**.

Halina: The cashier**'s not** here.

Dorota: It's a self checkout.

bar code

DID YOU KNOW?

Some people bring their own reusable bags to the supermarket. They use the bag many times. In some supermarkets, plastic bags aren't free.

Self-service checkout at a supermarket

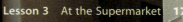

Vocabulary	Context
early	It's 8 a.m. It's **early**.
crowded	The store is empty. It isn't **crowded**.
parking lot	I am in the supermarket. My car is in the **parking lot**.
sure	I'm confused. I'm not **sure** what to do.
hard	It's not **hard** to use the supermarket. It's easy.
price	The **price** is 89¢ a pound.
product	The supermarket has many **products**: milk, fruit, meat.
shelf/shelves	The items are on the **shelves**.
bar code	A **bar code** is on each product. The cashier scans the bar code.
package	The cookies are in plastic **packages**.
the same	Prices aren't **the same** every week. They change.
on sale	Crackers are **on sale** this week. They're only $2.50 a box instead of $3.50.
pound	Americans use **pounds**, not kilograms. The abbreviation for pound is *lb*.
free	The packages of cookies aren't **free**. They're $2.79.
sample	The store has **samples** sometimes. You can try the product.
bag	I bring a reusable **bag** to the supermarket. I don't use paper or plastic **bags**.
cashier	The **cashiers** are at the checkouts. They use registers and give the customers their change.
self checkout	The **self checkout** is fast. The customer scans the items.

LISTEN

Listen to the sentences about the conversation. Circle *true* or *false*.

CD 1
TR 9

1. True   (False)   5. True   False
2. True   False   6. True   False
3. True   False   7. True   False
4. True   False

bag

1.6 *Be*—Negative Statements

PART A: Compare negative long forms and contractions.

Negative Long Forms	Negative Contractions	
I am not sure.	**I'm not** sure.	
You are not early.	**You're not** early.	**You aren't** early.
She is not a cashier.	**She's not** a cashier.	**She isn't** a cashier.
He is not at home.	**He's not** at home.	**He isn't** at home.
The store is not small.	**The store's not** small.	**The store isn't** small.
It is not crowded.	**It's not** crowded.	**It isn't** crowded.
That is not the price.	**That's not** the price.	**That isn't** the price.
We are not in the laundromat.	**We're not** in the laundromat.	**We aren't** in the laundromat.
They are not on sale.	**They're not** on sale.	**They aren't** on sale.
The cookies are not free.		**The cookies aren't** free.

Language Notes:

1. We cannot make a contraction for *am not*.

   NOT: I amn't sure.

2. We cannot make a contraction for a plural noun + *are*.

   NOT: The cookies're free.

PART B: Compare affirmative and negative statements with *be*.

Affirmative	Negative
We **are** at the supermarket.	We **aren't** at home.
The milk **is** fresh.	It **isn't** old.
I **am** new here.	I**'m not** sure about many things.
The samples **are** free.	The cookies in packages **aren't** free.
You **are** from the United States.	You**'re not** from Mexico.
Peter **is** a new immigrant.	Dorota **isn't** a new immigrant.

EXERCISE 1 Fill in the blanks with a negative form of the underlined form of *be*. Use contractions when possible.

1. The supermarket <u>is</u> big. It ___isn't OR 's not___ small.

2. The date <u>is</u> on packages. The date _____ on fruit.

3. We<u>'re</u> at the supermarket. We _____ at the laundromat.

4. Crackers <u>are</u> $2.50 this week. They _____ $2.50 every week.

5. I<u>'m</u> in the supermarket. I _____ in the laundromat.

6. The store <u>is</u> empty. It _____ crowded.

7. You<u>'re</u> helpful. You _____ confused. *continued*

8. Prices <u>are</u> on the shelves. They _____ on the products.

9. The sample cookies <u>are</u> free. The packages of cookies _____ free.

10. That's a bar code. That _____ the price.

EXERCISE 2 Check (✓) the true statements. Change the false statements to the negative form and add a true statement. Answers may vary.

1. _____ Supermarkets are dirty. *Supermarkets aren't dirty. They're clean.*

2. __✓__ Cashiers are helpful.

3. _____ I'm confused about supermarkets.

4. _____ Life in the United States is easy.

5. _____ Supermarkets are small.

6. _____ Americans are helpful.

7. _____ Supermarkets are crowded in the morning.

8. _____ Prices are the same every week.

9. _____ Supermarkets are hot.

10. _____ Bags are free.

1.7 Adjectives

Examples			Explanation
Subject	*Be*	**Adjective**	
The parking lot	is	**empty**.	An adjective can follow the verb *be*.
The store	isn't	**crowded**.	subject + *be* + (*not*) + adjective
The samples	are	**free**.	
Those are **free** samples.			An adjective can come before a noun.
These are **big** packages.			adjective + noun

Language Note:
Descriptive adjectives are always singular. Only the noun is plural.
    one **free** sample
    two **free** samples

EXERCISE 3 In each conversation, fill in the blanks with an adjective from the box.

CD 1
TR 10

CONVERSATION A: New immigrant, Lisa, and Dorota are at the supermarket.

| new ✓ | early | helpful | good |
| crowded | easy | big | different |

Lisa: I'm _____ new _____ to this country. Everything is _____ for me.
1.   2.

Dorota: Don't worry. I'm here with you.

Lisa: You're very _____.
3.

Dorota: This is the supermarket. It's _____ to shop in a supermarket.
4.

Lisa: The supermarket and the parking lot aren't _____. Why not?
5.

Dorota: It's only 10 a.m. It's _____.
6.

Lisa: This supermarket is _____. In my country, stores are small.
7.

Dorota: Look! Bananas are on sale this week. They're only 39¢ a pound. That's a _____ price.
8.

CONVERSATION B: Simon is showing Lisa's husband, Victor, the laundromat.

| small | open | different | hot | big |

Simon: This is the laundromat.

Victor: It's _____ in here.
9.

Simon: Yes, it is. But the door is _____.
10.

Victor: Some machines are _____ and some are _____.
11.   12.

Simon: The big machines are for big items, like blankets.

Victor: All of these machines are the same, but those are _____.
13.

Simon: These are washing machines. Those machines are dryers.

Victor: In my country, I am the washer and the air is the dryer!

1.8 Expressions with *It*

Examples	Explanation
It's hot in the laundromat. **It**'s cold outside. **It**'s sunny today. **It** isn't rainy.	We use *it* with weather or temperature.
It's 10 a.m. **It**'s early. **It** isn't late. **It**'s Tuesday. **It**'s morning/afternoon/night.	We use *it* with time.

EXERCISE 4 Fill in the blanks with one of the words from the box.

early ✓	sunny	late	cold	7 a.m.	hot

1. It's _____ *early* _____ . It's only _____ .
           a.   **b.**

2. It's _____ in the laundromat. Open the door.

3. It's _____ outside. Close the door.

4. It's _____ . I am tired.

5. It's _____ today. We're at the beach.

EXERCISE 5 About You Fill in the blanks to make true statements. Use the words from the box in Exercise 4 or your own ideas.

1. It's _____ today. It isn't _____ today.
         a. day of week   **b.** day of week

2. It's _____ outside.

3. It's _____ inside.

4. It's _____ .

1.9 Singular and Plural—Spelling Rules

Singular	Plural	Rule
coin dime dollar	coins dimes dollars	We add -s to form the plural of most nouns.
dish watch box dress	dishes watches boxes dresses	We add -es to make the plural of nouns that end in *sh, ch, x,* and *ss.*
family baby	families babies	We change the final *y* to *i* and add -es when a word ends in a consonant + *y.*
day toy	days toys	We add only -s when a word ends in a vowel + *y.*
shelf life	shelves lives	We take away final *f* or *fe* and add -ves.

Pronunciation Note:

Sometimes we need to pronounce an extra syllable. Listen to your teacher pronounce these words:

　　price—prices　　noise—noises　　page—pages

EXERCISE 6 Fill in the blanks with the plural form of the noun given.

1. The _____ cars _____ are in the parking lot.
　　　　　　　　car

2. The _____ are under the _____.
　　　　　a. price　　　　　　　　　　　　b. shelf

3. The _____ are in a blue box.
　　　　　match

4. It's Saturday and many _____ are at the supermarket.
　　　　　　　　　　　　　　family

5. The soap for washing _____ costs $2.89.
　　　　　　　　　　　　dish

6. The _____ are on sale this week. Those _____ are on sale.
　　　　a. cracker　　　　　　　　　　　　　　　　b. box

7. Some _____ are in the supermarket today.
　　　　　baby

8. Dorota speaks two _____: Polish and English.
　　　　　　　　　　　　language

WRITING

PART 1 Editing Advice

1. Use the correct form of *be*.

    > *are*
    > You ~~is~~ at the laundromat.

2. Every sentence has a subject.

    > *It's*
    > ~~Is~~ 10:15 a.m.
    >
    > *It's*
    > ~~Is~~ hot today.
    >
    > *He is*
    > This is Simon. ~~Is~~ from Mexico.

3. Don't confuse *this* and *these*.

    > *These*
    > ~~This~~ are big machines.
    >
    > *This*
    > ~~These~~ is my bank.

4. In a contraction, put the apostrophe in place of the missing letter.

    > *You're*
    > ~~Your'e~~ late.
    >
    > *isn't*
    > The supermarket ~~is'nt~~ crowded.

5. Use an apostrophe, not a comma, in a contraction.

    > *I'm*
    > ~~I,m~~ at the supermarket.

6. Don't make adjectives plural.

    > *big*
    > These are ~~bigs~~ machines.

7. Don't use *a* before a plural noun.

    > This is a small machine. Those are ~~a~~ big machines.

8. Don't confuse *your* and *you're*.

    > *You're*
    > ~~Your~~ at the supermarket.

9. Don't confuse *he* and *she*.

    > *She*
    > Dorota is from Poland. ~~He~~ is from Warsaw.
    >
    > *He*
    > Simon is from Mexico. ~~She~~ speaks Spanish.

PART 2 Editing Practice

Some of the shaded words and phrases have mistakes. Find the mistakes and correct them. If the shaded words are correct, write *C*.

Dorota and Lisa are in the laundromat.

> *We're*
> **Dorota:**   We,re here to wash clothes.
>   1.

Lisa: It's easy to wash clothes in a laundromat.
            C
            2.

Dorota: Yes, it is. But is hot in here.
              3.

Lisa: Your right.
            4.

Dorota: The door is'nt open.
              5.

Lisa: This are my blankets.
            6.

Dorota: Theyr'e big. Those machines is for bigs items. This machines are for small items. These are a
              7.   8.   9.   10.   11.   12.

quarters for the machines.

Lisa: Thanks. Your'e helpful.
            13.

Dorota: I,m here to help. Simon's helpful too. But is at the bank today. She's with Victor.
              14.   15.   16.

PART 3 Write About It

Rewrite the following paragraph. Change the singular nouns and pronouns to plurals. Change other necessary words too.

This is a green apple. It's on sale. It's very big. It's only $1.75 a pound. That's a red apple.

It isn't on sale. It's not very big. It's $2.39 a pound. This is a free sample of the green apple. It's

not very fresh. That's a free sample of the red apple. It's fresh. This red apple is good. That

green apple isn't good today.

   These are green apples.

PART 4 Learner's Log

1. Write one sentence about each of these topics. Write affirmative and negative sentences with *be*.
    - An American laundromat
    - An American supermarket
    - Items in an American supermarket

2. Write any questions you still have about the topics above.

Passengers run for their
trains at Grand Central Station

TIME AND MONEY

Time is more valuable than money. You can get more money, but you cannot get more time.

— Jim Rohn

1

GRAMMAR

Possessive Nouns
Possessive Adjectives

CONTEXT

Time

A clockmaker fixes a clock.

BEFORE YOU READ

Circle *yes* or *no*.

1. I wear a watch every day.　　　　Yes　　No

2. I have a clock in my bedroom.　　Yes　　No

READ

CD 1
TR 11

Read the following conversation. Pay special attention to the possessive forms in bold.

Victor and Dorota are in **Dorota's** car.

Victor: Hi, Dorota. I'm surprised to see you. It's **Simon's** turn to help me.

Dorota: Yes, it is. But he's with **his** kids[1] today. **His** wife, Marta, is at the hospital. **Her** father is sick. So I'm here to help you with the bank.

Victor: It's late. Look at **your** clock. It's 4:30. The bank is closed.

Dorota: No, it isn't. **My** clock is fast. It's only 4:15.

Victor: So **your** clock is broken.

Dorota: No, it isn't. **My** clock is always fast. And **my** watch is always fast too. That way I'm always on time.

Victor: I'm confused. **Your** clock is fast, and that's OK with you?

Dorota: Yes. I'm never late. Time is important for Americans. **Their** ideas about time are different from **our** ideas about time.

(five minutes later)

Dorota: We're here now. Oh, no. The bank is closed. Today is a holiday. It's the Fourth of July.

_____

[1] *Kid(s)* is informal. *Child(ren)* is formal.

DID YOU KNOW?
Some American holidays are: Memorial Day (May), Independence Day/Fourth of July (July), Labor Day (September), Columbus Day (October), and Thanksgiving (November).

Vocabulary	Context
surprised	Simon isn't here today. Victor is **surprised** to see Dorota.
turn	It's Simon's **turn** to help.
kid, son, daughter	Simon and Marta have three **kids**. They have a **son** and two **daughters**.
wife	Simon has a **wife**. Her name is Marta.
clock	Look at the **clock**. It's 4:30.
fast	Your clock is **fast**. It's only 4:15 but your clock says "4:30."
broken	My clock is **broken**. It doesn't work.
watch	I wear my **watch** on my wrist.
on time	You're **on time**. You're not late.
holiday	It's a **holiday** today. The schools and banks are closed.

LISTEN

Listen to the sentences about the conversation. Circle *true* or *false*.

1. (True)   False   5. True   False
2. True   False   6. True   False
3. True   False   7. True   False
4. True   False

2.1 Possessive Nouns

Examples	Explanation
Simon's wife is at the hospital. **Marta's** father is sick.	We use noun + *'s* to show relationship.
Dorota's clock is fast.	We use noun + *'s* to show ownership.

EXERCISE 1 Fill in the blanks with *Marta's, Simon's,* or *Dorota's.*

1. _____Dorota's_____ clock is fast.

2. Marta is _____ wife.

3. _____ father is sick. He's in the hospital.

4. Today it's _____ turn to help, but he's with the kids.

5. _____ first language is Polish.

6. _____ first language is Spanish. He's from Mexico.

EXERCISE 2 Fill in the blanks. Put the words given in the correct order. Add an apostrophe (') + *s* to make a possessive noun.

1. _____Simon's kids_____ aren't in school today.
        kids/Simon

2. _____ isn't with him.
        daughter/Victor

3. _____ are at home.
        Simon/children

4. _____ is sick.
        father/Marta

5. This is _____ .
        Dorota/car

2.2 Possessive Adjectives

Compare subject pronouns and possessive adjectives.

Subject Pronoun	Possessive Pronoun	Examples
I	my	**I** am late. **My** watch is slow.
You	your	**You** are late. **Your** watch is slow.
He	his	**He** is late. **His** watch is slow.
She	her	**She** is late. **Her** watch is slow.
We	our	**We** are late. **Our** clock is slow.
They	their	**They** are late. **Their** clock is slow.

EXERCISE 3 Fill in the blanks with *my, your, his, her, our,* or *their*.

1. You are with _____your_____ kids.

2. She is with _____ kids.

3. They are with _____ kids.

4. I am with _____ kids.

5. He is with _____ kids.

6. We are with _____ kids.

EXERCISE 4 About You Circle *true* or *false*.

1. My watch is fast.	True	False
2. Time is important to me.	True	False
3. Money is important to me.	True	False
4. My classmate's language is different from my language.	True	False
5. My teacher's name is hard for me to say.	True	False

 EXERCISE 5 Simon and Dorota are on the telephone. Fill in the blanks with *my, your, his, her, our,* or *their*.

CD 1
TR 13

Simon: Hi, Dorota. This is Simon. I'm busy today. Marta's busy too. _____Her_____ father is sick.
1.

_____ kids are at home today. _____ school is closed. It's _____ turn to help
2.   3.   4.

Victor today, but I'm busy.

Dorota: That's OK. _____ kids need you. I'm not busy today.
5.

2

View of the Brooklyn Bridge from inside a clock tower in Manhattan, NY

BEFORE YOU READ

Circle *yes* or *no*.

1.	I'm usually on time.	Yes	No
2.	My doctor is usually on time.	Yes	No

READ

Read the following conversation. Pay special attention to the *yes/no* questions in bold.

Simon comes to the bank to help Victor.

Simon: **Am I** late? Traffic is bad today.

Victor: You're not late. It's only 10:15.

Simon: Oh, I'm fifteen minutes late, then. I'm sorry.

Victor: Fifteen minutes is nothing.

Simon: In the United States, people are usually on time.

Victor: Really? **Are you** serious?

Simon: Yes, I am.

Victor: I'm surprised. **Are people** on time for everything?

Simon: For most things. They're on time for appointments.

Victor: **Is this** an appointment?

Simon: Yes, it is. I'm here to help you with the bank.

Victor: I'm confused. My doctor is never on time. She's always late.

Simon: That's different. Doctors are always late. They are very busy.

Victor: **Is it** necessary to be on time with friends?

Simon: It's not necessary, but it is polite.

Victor: Look. The time *and* temperature are on the clock outside the bank. **Is time** always on your mind?

Simon: Yes, it is. "Time is money." Time is always on our minds.

DID YOU KNOW?

Americans use Fahrenheit (F) for temperature. Other countries use Celsius (C).

Vocabulary	Context
traffic	There are a lot of cars. **Traffic** is bad today.
usually	Students are **usually** on time for class. They don't arrive late.
serious	Are you **serious**? Is it true?
appointment	Victor has a 10 a.m. **appointment** with Simon.
never	Some people are **never** on time. They are always late.
polite	It's **polite** to say "please" and "thank you."
temperature	The **temperature** is 69 degrees today.
outside/inside	Victor is in the parking lot. He is **outside** the bank. He isn't **inside** the bank.
on (my, your, etc.) mind	Time is always **on my mind**. I think about it a lot.
always	Lisa **always** goes to the supermarket on Mondays. She never goes on Tuesdays.

Fahrenheit	Celsius
0	−18
10	−12
20	−7
30	−1
40	4
50	10
60	16
70	21
80	27
90	32
100	38
212	100

LISTEN

Listen to the questions about the conversation. Circle the correct answer.

CD 1
TR 15

1. Yes, it is.   No, it isn't.   4. Yes, they are.   No, they aren't.

2. Yes, he is.   No, he isn't.   5. Yes, it is.   No, it isn't.

3. Yes, they are.   No, they aren't.   6. Yes, they are.   No, they aren't.

2.3 Be—Yes/No Questions

PART A: We put the form of *be* before the subject to ask a question.

Be	Subject		Short Answer
Am	I	late?	No, you aren't.
Is	traffic	bad?	Yes, it is.
Is	Simon	on time?	No, he isn't.
Are	you	serious?	Yes, I am.
Are	they	at the bank?	Yes, they are.

Language Note:

You can use a contraction for a negative answer. We don't use a contraction for an affirmative answer.

    No, you aren't. **OR** No, you're not.   Yes, you are.   NOT: Yes, you're.

Pronunciation Note:

A *yes/no* question has rising intonation. Listen to your teacher pronounce the statements and the questions above.

Punctuation Note:

We put a question mark (?) at the end of a question.

PART B: Compare statements and *yes/no* questions with *be*.

Statements	Yes/No Questions
I am late.	**Am I** very late?
Time is important.	**Is time** always on your mind?
Some people are on time.	**Are some people** always on time?
It is necessary to be on time.	**Is it** necessary to be on time with friends?

EXERCISE 1 Fill in the correct form of *be* and the noun or pronoun given to make a question.

1. _____Are Simon and Victor_____ at the supermarket? No, they aren't.

       Simon and Victor

2. _____ students? Yes, they are.

       they

3. _____ open? Yes, it is.

       the supermarket

4. _____ late? No, you're not.

       I

5. _____ good to be on time? Yes, it is.

       it

6. _____ inside the school? No, I'm not.

       you

7. _____ on time? Yes, we are.

       we

8. _____ polite? Yes, she is.

       Dorota

EXERCISE 2 Answer with a short answer, based on the conversation on page 33.

1. Is the bank open? _____ Yes, it is. _____

2. Is Simon on time? _____

3. Are Simon and Victor at the bank? _____

4. Is Simon with Dorota? _____

5. Are doctors usually on time? _____

6. Is it necessary to be on time with friends? _____

7. Is it polite to be on time with friends? _____

8. Are Americans usually late for appointments? _____

EXERCISE 3 About You Answer with a short answer. Share your answers with a partner.

1. Are you usually on time? _____ Yes, I am. _____

2. Are you surprised about some things in this country? _____

3. Is your apartment big? _____

4. Are you a serious student? _____

5. Are you an immigrant? _____

6. Are you a parent? _____

7. Are you on time for everything? _____

8. Is this class easy for you? _____

9. Is English hard for you? _____

10. Are your classmates always serious? _____

11. Is your teacher always on time? _____

12. Are people in this city usually polite? _____

CD 1
TR 16

EXERCISE 4 Fill in the blanks to complete the conversations. Use contractions when possible..

CONVERSATION A: Victor and Dorota are at the library.

Victor: _____Am I_____ on time?
1.

Dorota: Yes, you _____ .
2.

Victor: _____ at the library?
3.

Dorota: Yes, we _____ . We're here to learn about the library.
4.

Victor: _____ open?
5.

Dorota: No, it _____ . It's only 8:48. We're a few minutes early.
6.

CONVERSATION B: Simon and Marta are on the telephone.

Simon: Hello?

Marta: Hi, Simon.

Simon: _____ on your way home?
7.

Marta: No, I _____ . I'm at the supermarket now.
8.

Simon: _____ open now? It's 9 p.m.
9.

Marta: Yes, it _____ . This store is open
10.

twenty-four hours a day.

Simon: _____ with Halina still?
11.

Marta: No, I'm not. I'm alone now.

Simon: We need bananas. _____ on sale?
12.

Marta: Yes, they _____ . They're only 39¢ a
13.

pound this week.

Simon: Buy bread too. _____ also on sale?
14.

Marta: No, it _____ .
15.

2.4 Irregular Plural Forms

Singular	Plural	Explanation
child person	children people	Sometimes the plural form is a different word.
man woman	men women	Sometimes the plural form has a vowel change.

Pronunciation Note:

We can hear the difference between *woman* and *women* in the first syllable. Listen to your teacher pronounce the singular and plural forms above.

EXERCISE 5 Fill in the blanks with the singular or plural form of the noun given.

1. The _____ *men* _____ are at the bank.

        man

2. One _____ is behind me. Two _____ are in front of me.

     a. person   **b.** person

3. The _____ is with three _____ .

     a. woman   **b.** child

4. One _____ is small. The other _____ are not small.

     a. child   **b.** child

5. A _____ is behind me.

     man

6. Five _____ are in line.

     woman

7. Three _____ are near the door.

     man

EXERCISE 6 Fill in the blanks with the correct form of *be*.

1. The people at the bank _____ *are* _____ helpful.

2. This child _____ with her mother.

3. Those children _____ with their father.

4. The woman _____ busy.

5. One person _____ alone.

6. The people in the bank _____ busy.

7. That man _____ polite.

behind

in front of

3

A woman uses an automated teller machine (ATM).

BEFORE YOU READ

Circle *yes* or *no*.

1. I have a bank account.   Yes   No

2. I have an ATM card.   Yes   No

Read the following conversation. Pay special attention to the *wh-* questions and articles *a* and *an* in bold.

Dorota and Victor are at the bank.

Dorota: Hi, Victor. **How are you?**

Victor: Hi, Dorota. I'm fine, thanks. **Where is Simon?**

Dorota: He's at the supermarket already.

Victor: Is this your bank?

Dorota: Yes, it is.

Victor: **What time is it?**

Dorota: It's 7:30 p.m. The bank is closed now. We can't go inside.

Victor: **Who's that woman** over there?

Dorota: She's a security guard.

Victor: **When is the bank** open?

Dorota: This bank is open from 9 to 4, Monday through Thursday. It's open from 9 to 7 on Friday and 9 to 1 on Saturday.

Victor: **Why are we** here, then?

Dorota: I'm out of cash. I need cash for the supermarket. The ATM is always open.

Victor: **What's an ATM? A** cash machine?

Dorota: **An** ATM is **an** Automated Teller Machine. And yes, it's **a** machine for cash.

Victor: **What's that?** Your bank card?

Dorota: Yes, it opens the door. And I use it to get cash. I need **a** PIN for my account too.

Victor: **What's a PIN?**

Dorota: It's **a** Personal Identification Number.

Victor: **What's your PIN?**

Dorota: That's **a** secret!

DID YOU KNOW?
You can use mobile or online banking services to save time. You can see your monthly statement and pay bills.

Vocabulary	Context
security guard	The **security guard** works at the bank.
through	The bank is open Monday **through** Saturday.
out of	I'm **out of** money. I don't have any money.
cash	We are at the bank. It's easy to get **cash** at an ATM.
ATM	The **ATM** is an easy way to get money.
automated	It's **automated**. A computer makes it work.
teller	A **teller** works at a bank.
PIN	A **PIN** is a Personal Identification Number.
account	I have a bank **account** for my savings.
secret	No one knows my PIN. It's a **secret.**

LISTEN

Listen to the questions about the conversation. Circle the correct answer.

CD 1
TR 18

1. At the bank   At the supermarket

2. Dorota's   Simon's

3. Yes, it's late.   It's 7:30.

4. She's a bank teller.   She's a security guard.

5. twenty-four hours a day   Monday through Saturday

6. from 9 a.m. to 4 p.m.   twenty-four hours a day

7. It's a machine for cash.   It's at the bank.

8. at 10:15   to get cash

9. 924   It's a secret.

2.5 Be—Wh- Questions

PART A: Wh- questions begin with *where, when, why, who, what, whose,* and *how*. Observe the word order in a *wh-* question. *Wh-* questions are also called *information questions*.

Question Word(s)	Be	Subject		Answer
Where	are	we?		We're at the bank.
What	is	that?		It's an ATM.
What time	is	it?		It's 10:15.
Why	are	we	here?	We're here to get cash.
When	is	the bank	open?	It's open Monday through Saturday.
Who	is	that woman?		She's a security guard.
Whose money	is	this?		It's Dorota's money.
How	are	you?		I'm fine, thanks.
How old	is	Simon's son?		He's 15 (years old).

Language Note:

We can make a contraction with most *wh-* words and *is*.

> **What's** an ATM?   **When's** the bank open?   **Why's** he here?

PART B: Compare statements and *wh-* questions.

Statements	Wh- Questions
The bank is open.	When **is the bank** open?
We are at the ATM.	Why **are we** at the ATM?
You are a student.	How old **are you**?
I am at a bank.	Where **am I**?
She is inside the bank.	Why **is she** inside the bank?
Dorota is an immigrant.	Who **is Dorota**?
That is Dorota's money.	Whose money **is that**?
It is late.	What time **is it**?

Pronunciation Note:

Wh- questions have a falling intonation.

> Where is the bank?

Listen to your teacher pronounce the statements and questions above.

EXERCISE 1 Fill in the blanks with a question word to complete this conversation between Dorota and Lisa.

Dorota: _____How_____ are you?
1.

Lisa: I'm fine. _____ are we?
2.

Dorota: We're at the bank.

Lisa: _____'s that?
3.

Dorota: It's an ATM.

Lisa: _____ are we here?
4.

Dorota: To learn about the bank.

Lisa: _____'s that woman?
5.

Dorota: She's the security guard.

Lisa: _____ is the bank open?
6.

Dorota: Monday through Thursday, from 9 a.m. to 4 p.m., Friday from 9 a.m. to 7 p.m.,

and Saturday from 9 a.m. to 1 p.m.

Lisa: _____ is it?
7.

Dorota: It's 8:45. We're early.

EXERCISE 2 Complete the questions.

1. It's late. What time _____is it_____?

2. We're late. Why _____?

3. The ATM is near here. Where _____?

4. That woman is in the bank. Who _____?

5. That money is Dorota's. Whose _____ this?

6. Simon's 42 years old. How _____ Marta?

EXERCISE 3 About You Answer the questions.

1. What time is it now? _____

2. Where are you from? _____

3. Who's your English teacher? _____

4. How old are you? _____

continued

5. Where's your school? _____

6. When's the school open? _____

7. Who's your friend? _____

8. Where's your English book? _____

2.6 Articles *A* and *An*

We use *a* or *an* before a singular noun.

Examples	Explanation
What's this? It's **a** bank. Who's that woman? She's **a** security guard.	We use *a* before a consonant sound.
What's that? It's **an** ATM. What's this? It's **an** envelope.	We use *an* before a vowel sound. The vowels are *a, e, i, o,* and *u*.
Quarters and dimes are coins. What are those? They're pennies.	We don't use *a* or *an* before a plural noun. Not: Quarters and dimes are *a* coins. Not: Those are *a* pennies.
adjective adjective + noun The bank is big. It's **a** big bank.	We use *a* or *an* only if a noun follows the adjective. Not: The bank is *a* big.

EXERCISE 4 Fill in the blanks with *a* or *an*.

1. This is __*a*__ bank.

2. That's __*an*__ envelope.

3. I'm _____ immigrant.

4. I'm _____ new immigrant.

5. You are _____ helpful person.

6. This is _____ new book.

7. A quarter is _____ coin.

8. Dorota isn't _____ old woman.

9. Simon's from Mexico. Mexico is _____ North American country.

10. He's _____ busy person.

EXERCISE 5 Rewrite the sentence with the adjective given. Change *a* to *an* or *an* to *a* if needed.

1. First Community is a bank. <u>First Community is an old bank.</u>
   old

2. That's an ATM. _____
   new

3. Thanksgiving is a holiday. _____
   American

4. This is a number. _____
   identification

5. This is a test. _____
   easy

6. That's an envelope. _____
   big

🎧 **EXERCISE 6** Fill in the blanks with the correct form of *be* and *a* or *an* where necessary.
CD 1
TR 20 Use contractions when possible.

Halina: What's that?

Simon: It <u>'s an</u> _____ ATM.
           　　　1.

Halina: What's an ATM?

Simon: It _____ machine for cash.
           　　2.

Halina: What are these?

Simon: These _____ envelopes for checks.
           　　　3.

Halina: What _____ check?
           　　4.

Simon: Look. This _____ check. It _____ paycheck from my work.
           　　　　5.　　　　　　　　6.

Halina: What _____ those?
           　　7.

Simon: Those _____ drive-up ATMs.
           　　　8.

Halina: Americans _____ very busy. They _____ always in their cars.
            　　　　　　9.　　　　　　　　　10.

Simon: It _____ easy way to use the bank. It's fast too!
           　　　11.

A man at a drive-up ATM

WRITING

PART 1 Editing Advice

1. *People* is a plural word. Use a plural verb.

   The new people ~~is~~ *are* late.

2. Use the correct possessive adjective.

   She is with ~~his~~ *her* father.

   They are with ~~they~~ *their* mother.

3. Don't confuse *you're* and *your*.

   What's ~~you're~~ *your* name?

   ~~Your~~ *You're* never late.

4. Use the correct word order in a question.

   Why ~~you are~~ *are you* late?

   Is ~~big the supermarket~~ *the supermarket big*?

5. Use *a* or *an* before a singular noun.

   This is *a* bank. It's *an* old bank.

6. Don't use *a* or *an* with plural nouns.

   Victor and Dorota are ~~an~~ immigrants.

7. Use *a*, not *an*, before a vowel sound.

   She is ~~a~~ *an* immigrant.

8. Use the correct plural form.

   The ~~childs~~ *children* are happy.

9. Use the correct possessive form with nouns.

   Dorota *'s* clock is fast.

PART 2 Editing Practice

Some of the shaded words and phrases have mistakes. Find the mistakes and correct them. If the shaded words are correct, write *C*.

Ali and Simon are at the bank.

Ali: *C* Are we at your bank?
             1.

Simon: Yes, we're at my bank. What time ~~it is~~ *is it*?
                                                 2.

Ali: It's 9:15. Why we are here?
                       3.

Simon:	To learn about the ATM.
Ali:	What's a ATM? 4.
Simon:	It's machine for cash. 5.
Ali:	Where's Dorota today? Why she isn't here? 6. 7.
Simon:	His son is home. She's with him. 8. 9.
Ali:	Is small her son? 10.
Simon:	No, he's not. He's an young man. 11. 12.
Ali:	How old is Dorota son? 13.
Simon:	He's 18 years old. He's a college student. 14.
Ali:	Oh, look. The bank's closed today. 15.
Simon:	Don't worry. I have a card to use the ATM. 16.
Ali:	Why is those people in the bank? The bank is closed but those person are inside. 17. 18.
Simon:	They're a security guards. 19.
Ali:	Your right. 20.

PART 3 Write About It

Look at the picture. Write five *yes/no* and *wh-* questions about Marta and her daughter, Amy. Answer the questions.

Where are Marta and Amy? They're at the doctor's office.

PART 4 Learner's Log

1. Complete the following sentences with your own ideas.

   a. People are on time for _____ .

   b. _____ are at banks.

   c. An ATM is _____ .

2. Write any questions you still have about the topics above.

Thorp's image of tweets with the words *just landed* sent in a 36-hour period.

SENDING
INFORMATION

Everything that someone else measures
about you, you actually own.

—Jer Thorp

1

GRAMMAR

Imperatives—Affirmative

Imperatives—Negative

CONTEXT

Getting a Social Security Card

BEFORE YOU READ

Circle *yes* or *no.*

1. I have a Social Security card.   Yes   No

2. I write the month before the day.   Yes   No

   (For example: October 27 or 10/27)

READ

Read the following conversation. Pay special attention to imperative forms in bold.

Dorota: I have something for you. **Look.**

Halina: What is it?

Dorota: It's an application. It's for a Social Security card.

Halina: I'm not sure what to do.

Dorota: **Don't worry.** It's easy. **Let** me help.

Halina: OK. I have a pencil.

Dorota: No, no. **Don't use** a pencil. **Use** a blue or black pen.

Halina: OK.

Dorota: Here's a pen. **Fill out** all the information. **Print** the information, but **sign** your name in item 17.

Halina: I'm finished.

Dorota: What's your date of birth?

Halina: 11/6/80.

Dorota: Is your birthday in November?

Halina: No. It's in June.

Dorota: **Don't write** 11/6. **Write** the month, then the day. That's the way we write the date in the United States.

Halina: OK. 6/11/80.

Dorota: **Don't write** 80. **Write** 1980.

Halina: Okay. I'm finished. What's next?

Dorota: **Don't forget** to sign your name. **Make** a copy of your birth certificate. Then **go** to the Social Security office. **Take** your birth certificate and another identity document with you.

DID YOU KNOW?

Identity documents include:
- driver's licenses
- marriage certificates
- passports
- school IDs (identification cards)
- birth certificates
- state-issued IDs

Vocabulary	Context
application	This is an **application** for a Social Security card. Please write your information.
let	**Let** me help you. I can answer your questions.
fill out	**Fill out** the application with a pen. Please complete it.
information	The application has a lot of questions. Write the **information** on the line.
print	**Print** your name. Halina Laski
sign	**Sign** your name. *Halina Laski*
birthday/date of birth	Ali's **birthday/date of birth** is April 3, 1985.
forget	**Don't forget** your Social Security number. It's an important identification number to remember.
copy	This is my original birth certificate. That is a **copy**.
birth certificate	A new baby gets a **birth certificate**.
identity document	My driver's license is an **identity document**. It says who I am.

LISTEN

CD 1
TR 22

Listen to these instructions about how to fill out a Social Security card application. Circle *true* or *false*.

1. (True)   False   5. True   False

2. True   False   6. True   False

3. True   False   7. True   False

4. True   False   8. True   False

3.1 Imperatives—Affirmative

We use the base form of the verb for the imperative.

Examples	Explanation
Use a pen. **Write** your date of birth.	We use the imperative to give instructions or suggestions.
Look at this.	We use the imperative to get someone's attention.
Help me, *please*. *Please* **help** me.	We add *please* to be more polite.

A line forms outside a Social Security office.

EXERCISE 1 Match the parts of the sentences to make an affirmative imperative.

1. Make _____b_____
2. Fill _____
3. Go _____
4. Use _____
5. Write _____
6. Take _____
7. Sign _____
8. I'm confused. Help _____

a. your birth certificate with you.
b. a copy of your birth certificate. ✓
c. a pen.
d. to the social security office today.
e. the month before the day.
f. me, please.
g. out the application today.
h. your name in item 17.

3.2 Imperatives—Negative

Examples	Explanation
Don't worry. **Don't write** 11/6 for June 11. **Don't be** late.	We use *don't* + the base form for the negative imperative. *Don't* is the contraction for *do not*.

EXERCISE 2 Rewrite the sentences. Use the negative imperative.

1. Forget your papers at home. _Don't forget your papers at home._____

2. Be late for your meeting. _____

3. Use a red pen. _____

4. Print your name. _____

5. Leave item 17 empty. _____

6. Write the day first. _____

7. Write with a pencil. _____

8. Go to the Social Security office on Sunday. _____

EXERCISE 3 Fill in the blanks with an affirmative or negative imperative. Use the verbs from the box. Answers may vary.

use	put	get	forget	write	take

1. _____Don't get_____ the application dirty.

2. _____ a pencil to fill out your application.

3. _____ to sign your application at the end.

4. _____ two forms of ID with you to the Social Security office.

5. _____ all four numbers for the year (1980, not 80).

6. _____ the day first in your date of birth.

EXERCISE 4 Marta and Amy are in the kitchen. Fill in the blanks in their conversation with one of the verbs from the box. You can use some items more than once.

CD 1
TR 23

don't ask	don't forget	don't touch	wash	say
tell	make	let	be	get

Amy: _____Make_____ me a sandwich, Mommy.
        1.

Marta: I'm busy now. Later.

Amy: What's that?

Marta: It's my application. Your hands are dirty. _____ the application.
                                                          2.

Amy: What's an application? And what's that?

Marta: An application is an important form. And this is my birth certificate.

Please _____ so many questions. I'm busy now.
        3.

Amy: I'm thirsty. Please _____ me a glass of milk.
                              4.

Marta: Later. _____ quiet now, please, and _____ me finish.
                  5.   6.

This is very important.... OK. I'm finished now. How can I help you? Please _____ me.
                                                                              7.

Amy: _____ me a sandwich.
         8.

Marta: _____ , "Please."
           9.

Amy: Please.

Marta: And _____ your hands. _____ to use soap!
               10.   11.

Amy: Ok.

2

GRAMMAR
Let's—Affirmative and Negative
Subject and Object Pronouns

CONTEXT
Applying for Financial Aid

A student looks at her
financial aid paperwork.

BEFORE YOU READ

Circle *yes* or *no.*

1. It's easy to get financial aid.   Yes   No

2. Online forms are easy.   Yes   No

READ

CD 1
TR 24

Read the following conversation. Pay special attention to the subject and object pronouns and *let's* + the base form in bold.

Halina and Shafia are students at the same school.

Halina: College is expensive in the United States.

Shafia: **You**'re right.

Halina: **Let's go** to the financial aid office on campus tomorrow. **Let's get** an application for financial aid.

Shafia: That's not necessary. **Let's go** on the Internet and get an application.

Halina: Is the application online?

Shafia: Yes. **Let me** show **you**. Look!

Halina: **You**'re right. Here's the financial aid website. The application is here.

Shafia: **Let's fill out** the application online. **It**'s easy. First, enter your Social Security number. Don't use dashes.

Halina: OK. What's next?

Shafia: Now enter your first and last name. Then, create a password.

Halina: OK. Don't look at my password. What about this question? What's a middle initial?

Shafia: I don't know. **Let's call** Dorota.

Halina: It's late. **Let's not bother her**. **I** know what *middle* means. **Let's look up** *initial* in the dictionary.

Shafia: OK. **Let's see**. **It** says, "the first letter of a name." So your middle initial is the first letter of your middle name.

DID YOU KNOW?

FAFSA (Free Application for Federal Student Aid) forms become available January 1. It's important to fill out your form as soon as possible.

July 1, 2015 – June 30, 2016

FAFSA®
FREE APPLICATION for FEDERAL STUDENT AID

Federal Student Aid | PROUD SPONSOR of the AMERICAN MIND®
An OFFICE of the U.S. DEPARTMENT of EDUCATION

Use this form to apply free for federal and state student grants, work-study, and loans.

Or apply free online at **www.fafsa.gov**.

Applying by the Deadlines

For federal aid, submit your application as early as possible, but no earlier than January 1, 2015. We must receive your application no later than June 30, 2016. Your college must have your correct, complete information by your last day of enrollment in the 2015-2016 school year.

For state or college aid, the deadline may be as early as January 2015. See the table to the right for state deadlines. You may also need to complete additional forms.

Check with your high school guidance counselor or a financial aid administrator at your college about state and college sources of student aid and deadlines.

If you are filing close to one of these deadlines, we recommend you file online at **www.fafsa.gov**. This is the fastest and easiest way to apply for aid.

Using Your Tax Return

We recommend that you complete and submit your FAFSA as soon as possible on or after January 1, 2015. If you (or your parents) need to file a 2014 income tax return with the Internal Revenue Service (IRS), and have not done so yet, you can submit your FAFSA *after* ~~estimated~~ tax information, and then you **must correct** that information

APPLICATION DEADLINES
Federal Aid Deadline - June 30, 2016
State Aid Deadlines - See below.

Check with your financial aid administrator for these states and territories:
AL, AS *, AZ, CO, FM *, GA, GU *, HI *, MH *, MP *, NE, NH *, NM, NV *, OH *, PR, PW *, SD *, TX, UT, VA *, VI *, WI and WY *.

Pay attention to the symbols that may be listed after your state deadline.

AK	Alaska Performance Scholarship - June 30, 2015 Alaska Education Grant - As soon as possible after January 1, 2015. Awards made until funds are depleted. Academic Challenge - June 1, 2015 *(date received)*
AR	Workforce Grant - Contact the financial aid office. Higher Education Opportunity Grant - June 1, 2015 *(date received)*
CA	For many state financial aid programs - March 2, 2015 *(date postmarked)* + * For additional community college Cal Grants - September 2, 2015 *(date postmarked)* + * Contact the California Student Aid Commission or your financial aid administrator for more information.
CT	February 15, 2015 *(date received)* # *
DC	FAFSA completed by April 1, 2015 For DCTAG, complete the DC OneApp and submit supporting documents by April 30, 2015.
DE	April 15, 2015 *(date received)*
FL	May 15, 2015 *(date processed)* Earlier priority deadlines may
IA	July 1, 2015 *(date received)* exist for certain programs. * Opportunity Grant - March 1, 2015 *(date received)* # *
ID	As soon as possible after January 1, 2015. Awards made until funds are depleted.
IL	

Vocabulary	Context
expensive	College is **expensive** in the United States. It costs a lot of money for many students.
financial aid	**Financial aid** is money to help pay for college.
online	The application is available **online**. It's on the Internet.
enter	**Enter** your name on Line 3 of the application.
dash	A **dash** is a short line. Social security numbers have **dashes** between numbers: 000-00-0000
create a password	**Create a password**. It's a secret number or word. My **password** has letters and numbers.
what about	**What about** this question? What is it?
initial	My name is Dorota Romana Nowak. My middle **initial** is R.
bother	He's busy. Let's not **bother** him.
look up	**Look up** *financial* in the dictionary. I want to know the meaning.

LISTEN

CD 1
TR 25

Listen to the sentences about the conversation. Circle *true* or *false*.

1. (True)   False   5. True   False

2. True   False   6. True   False

3. True   False   7. True   False

4. True   False   8. True   False

3.3 *Let's*—Affirmative and Negative

Examples	Explanation
Let's go to the office. **Let's get** an application.	We use *let's* + the base form to make a suggestion. *Let's* is the contraction for *let us*.
Let's not call now.	We use *let's not* + the base form to make the negative.

EXERCISE 1 Fill in the blanks with *let's* or *let's not* and one of the verbs from the box.

walk	fill it out	go✓	look up
get	call	drive	bother

1. _____Let's go_____ to the financial aid office today. I have a question about the form.

2. _____ to the financial aid office. It's far.

continued

3. It's very cold today. _____ there.

4. It's not necessary to go to the office. _____ the application online.

5. This application is easy. _____ now.

6. What's the application deadline? Where's the phone? _____ Dorota.

7. It's late. _____ her now.

8. I don't know what *password* means. _____ the word in the dictionary.

3.4 Subject and Object Pronouns

Compare subject pronouns and object pronouns.

Examples	Explanation	
	Subject Pronoun	**Object Pronoun**
I am confused. Please help **me**.	I	me
You are not alone. I am here to help **you**.	you	you
He is at home. Call **him**.	he	him
She is at home. Call **her**.	she	her
It is your date of birth. Write **it**.	it	it
We are busy. Don't bother **us**.	we	us
They are confused. Help **them**.	they	them
I am confused. Please help **me**.	We put the subject pronoun before the verb. We put the object pronoun after the verb.	
I am finished **with** it. This application is **for** you. This question is **about** me.	We use the object pronoun after a preposition. Some prepositions are: *with, for, about, to, on, in, of, at,* and *from.*	

EXERCISE 2 Fill in the blanks with an object pronoun.

1. I'm confused. Please help _____ me _____ .

2. Dorota is helpful. Let's call _____ .

3. I'm busy. Don't bother _____ .

4. We are confused. Please help _____ .

5. Simon is busy. Don't bother _____ .

6. I'm busy. Your father is here. Ask _____ for help.

7. Dorota and Simon are helpful. Let's ask _____ .

8. The application is necessary. Let's fill _____ out.

9. This is my password. Don't look at _____ .

10. Are you confused? Don't worry. I'm here to help _____ .

EXERCISE 3 Fill in the blanks with an object or subject pronoun.

1. Victor is our friend. _____*We*_____ call him with questions. He answers _____*them*_____ .
                    a.   **b.**

2. We help each other. I am here to help you. _____ are here to help _____ .
                    a.   **b.**

3. Dorota helps immigrants. _____ are often confused and ask _____ questions.
                    a.   **b.**

4. Mr. Adams teaches Halina. _____ is her teacher. She likes _____ a lot.
                    a.   **b.**

5. The questions are difficult. I don't understand _____ . They confuse _____ .
                    a.   **b.**

6. Ali and I are new. Please don't ask _____ any questions. _____ don't know the answers.
                    a.   **b.**

EXERCISE 4 Ali and Shafia are at home. Fill in the blanks in their conversation with an object or subject pronoun.

CD 1
TR 26

Ali: What's that?

Shafia: _____*It*_____ 's a financial aid application. College is expensive in the United States.
1.

We're immigrants. It's very expensive for _____ .
                                                              2.

Ali: It's expensive for Americans too. But it's easy for _____ to fill out the
                                                             3.

application. It isn't easy for _____ . This question is hard. I'm confused
                                             4.

about _____ . Let's call Dorota.
              5.

Shafia: _____ 's late. It's after 10 p.m. Maybe _____ 's asleep.
              6.   **7.**

Let's call _____ tomorrow.
                    8.

Ali: Or call Simon.

Shafia: _____ 's busy. His wife's father is sick. She's with _____ in the hospital.
              9.   **10.**

Simon's with his kids. He's with _____ all day.
                                         11.

Ali: Let's read the application together. Maybe _____ can do _____ together.
                                                  12.   **13.**

Shafia: Yes, let's try!

WRITING

PART 1 Editing Advice

1. Use *not* after *let's* to make the negative.

             not
    Let's ~~don't~~ be late.

2. Don't use *to* after *don't*.

    Don't ~~to~~ write on this line.

3. Don't use *to* after *let's*.

    Let's ~~to~~ eat now.

4. Don't forget the apostrophe in *let's*.

    Let's
    ~~Lets~~ go home.

5. Use the subject pronoun before the verb.

    They
    ~~Them~~ are good students.

6. Use the object pronoun after the verb or preposition.

             him
    Don't bother ~~he~~.

             them
    Look at ~~they~~.

PART 2 Editing Practice

Some of the shaded words and phrases have mistakes. Find the mistakes and correct them. If the shaded words are correct, write *C*.

Peter: Let's ~~to~~ call Dorota for help with the application. *C* She is always helpful to us.
              1.   **2.**   **3.**

Halina: Dorota is busy today. Her brother is sick. She's with he. Let's don't
                                                  4.   **5.**

              bother her now.

Peter: Maybe Simon is available. Let's call him.
                                      6.   **7.**

Halina: Don't to call him now. Marta's father is still sick. She is with him at the hospital.
              8.   **9.**

              Simon is with their kids. Dorota and Simon are both busy today.

Peter: You're right. Let's not to bother they.
                              10.   **11.**

Halina: Lets try to fill out the application together. The application is online.
              12.

              Let's print her.
                      13.

Peter: Make two copies, please. One is for you and one is for I.
              14.   **15.**   **16.**

Halina: OK.

PART 3 Write About It

Rewrite the following paragraph. Change all the underlined nouns to object pronouns.

> This is a financial aid application. Read <u>the financial aid application</u> carefully. Write your name and Social Security number on <u>the financial aid application</u>. Dashes are always in a Social Security number. Don't write <u>the dashes</u> on the application. Some questions are hard. Ask about <u>hard questions</u>. Dorota is helpful. Ask <u>Dorota</u> for help. The man at the financial aid office is helpful too. Ask <u>the man</u> for help. <u>The man</u> helps people.

This is a financial aid application. Read it carefully...

PART 4 Learner's Log

1. These seven steps for how to get a Social Security card are out of order. Write the number of the step to put them in order. Then rewrite the steps in the correct order.

   _____ Make a copy of your birth certificate.

   _____ Find another identity document.

   _____ Take or send all your documents to the Social Security office.

   _____ Don't forget to sign the form.

   _____ Get an application online or from the Social Security office.

   _____ Fill out all the necessary information.

   _____ Print the information.

2. Write one affirmative and one negative direction for each of these topics.
   - To fill out a Social Security card application.
   - To fill out a financial aid application.

3. Write any questions you still have about the topics above.

UNIT

4 Lifestyles

Visitors watch kayakers and manatees at Three Sisters Springs, Florida.

Happiness is not a matter of intensity but of balance, order, rhythm and harmony.

— Thomas Merton

1

CONTEXT

Free-Time Activities

Tyrannosaurus rex teeth at the North Carolina Museum of Natural Sciences in Raleigh, North Carolina

BEFORE YOU READ

1. What are your free-time activities?

2. What is your favorite summer activity?

READ

CD 1
TR 27

Read the following blog about free-time activities in the United States. Pay special attention to the simple present verbs and frequency words in bold.

Americans **work** hard. But they **have** fun too. Americans **do** many different activities in their free time. They **often visit** each other. But a visitor **usually needs** an invitation. Or the visitor **calls** first.

People **sometimes invite** their friends to their homes. **Sometimes**, they **eat** dinner together. Other times, they **watch** sports on TV together. One popular game is the Super Bowl. The two best football teams in the United States **play** in January or February every year.

Americans **like** the movies. They **often go** to the movies on weekends. Theaters **sell** popcorn and other snacks. People **buy** these treats at a concession stand.[1]

Americans also **enjoy** museums. Families **spend** time at the exhibits. Museums **have** interesting activities too. A list of activities is **usually** on a museum's website.

City parks **have** many fun activities too. In the summer, many city parks **have** free outdoor concerts. People **sometimes have** picnics. They **cook** on a grill and **eat** out side. They **call** this kind of food "barbecue." It's very popular.

Americans **enjoy** their free time.

_____
[1] Theaters and stadiums have *concession stands*. They sell drinks and snacks.

DID YOU KNOW?
Many theaters have cheaper tickets before 3 p.m. Senior citizens, children, and students may also get a discount.

Vocabulary	Context
have fun	I **have fun** at the museum. I am happy there.
activity	City parks often have free **activities**, or things to do.
free time	Dorota works in the daytime. She has **free time** at night.
visit (v.) visitor (n.)	Simon's friends often **visit** him. They come to his house. They are **visitors**.
each other	We visit **each other**. I visit you, and you visit me.
invitation (n.) invite (v.)	Americans ask their friends to visit. This is an **invitation.** Do you want to **invite** your friend to the house?
popular	Many people like football. It's a **popular** sport.
best	This book is better than those books. It's the **best**.
team	One football **team** has many players. They play together.
enjoy	Simon and Victor like football. They **enjoy** the Super Bowl.
spend time	Tina **spends** a lot of **time** with her friends. They are always together.
exhibit	The museum has a new art **exhibit**.
outdoor concert	I like **outdoor concerts**. I listen to music in the park.
cook	My father often **cooks** on a grill in the summer.

LISTEN

CD 1
TR 28

Listen to the sentences about the blog. Circle *true* or *false*.

1. (True)	False		5. True	False
2. True	False		6. True	False
3. True	False		7. True	False
4. True	False		8. True	False

4.1 The Simple Present—Affirmative Statements

A simple present verb has two forms: the base form and the *-s* form.

Subject	Verb (Base Form)	
I	**like**	concerts.
You	**have**	a grill.
We	**watch**	football games.
Americans	**enjoy**	movies.
They	**buy**	popcorn at the movies.

Subject	Verb (*-s* Form)	
Simon	**enjoys**	the Super Bowl.
He	**likes**	sports.
Lisa	**has**	a lot of friends.
She	**visits**	them on weekends.
My family	**spends**	a lot of time in the park.
Our team	**plays**	every Saturday.
It	**has**	good players.

Language Notes:

1. *Have* is an irregular verb. The *-s* form is *has*.

2. *Family* and *team* are singular nouns. We use the *-s* form of the verb with these nouns.

EXERCISE 1 Fill in the blanks with the correct form of the simple present. Use the verb given.

1. Simon _____*enjoys*_____ movies on the weekends.
   enjoy

2. His kids _____ activities in parks.
   like

3. Simon's family _____ fun together.
   have

4. His daughter often _____ her friends to play.
   invite

5. We _____ time with our friends.
   spend

6. Americans _____ before a visit to a friend's house.
   call

7. I _____ museums with my friends.
   visit

8. The best teams _____ in the Super Bowl.
   play

4.2 Spelling of the -s Form

Base Form	-s Form	Explanation
visit like see	visit**s** like**s** see**s**	We add -s to most verbs to make the -s form.
kiss wash watch fix	kiss**es** wash**es** watch**es** fix**es**	We add -es to base forms with ss, sh, ch, or x at the end.
do go	do**es** go**es**	We add -es to *do* and *go*.
worry try	worr**ies** tr**ies**	If the base form ends in a consonant + y, we change the y to an i and add -es.
pay play	pay**s** play**s**	If the base form ends in a vowel + y, we do not change the y. We just add -s.

Pronunciation Notes:

1. When we add -es to base forms with *ss, sh, ch,* or *x* at the end, we pronounce the extra syllable.

2. The pronunciation of *does* is /dʌz/. See Appendix A on page AP1 for more information about vowel and consonant sounds in English.

EXERCISE 2 Fill in the blanks with the -s form of the verb given.

1. The team _____plays_____ football.
   play

2. Each football team _____ hard.
   try

3. Simon's son, Ed, _____ football on TV.
   watch

4. He _____ football games.
   like

5. He sometimes _____ to football games.
   go

6. A football player sometimes _____ before a big game.
   worry

7. Simon _____ the grill after a barbecue.
   clean

continued

2

GRAMMAR

The Simple Present—Negative Statements

Time Expressions with the Simple Present

Infinitives with Simple Present Verbs

CONTEXT

Work

A man rakes cranberries in Wisconsin Rapids, Wisconsin.

BEFORE YOU READ

1. What's a good job?

2. What's a hard job?

READ

Read the following blog. Pay special attention to the negative forms of the simple present, time expressions, and infinitives in bold.

Work is very important to Americans. They often ask each other about their jobs. But they **don't ask** each other, "How much money do you make?" They **don't talk** about their wages or salaries.

Americans usually work **five days a week**. Many people get paid **every two weeks**. Most office workers and teachers **don't work on Saturdays and Sundays**. But many people have other days off. Workers in stores and restaurants hardly ever have days off **on weekends**. Stores and restaurants are very busy **on Saturdays and Sundays**.

Full-time work is usually **eight hours a day**, or **forty hours a week**, but many Americans work more. Some people complain about their hours. They **don't like to work** so much. But others want **to make** more money. People with hourly wages get extra money for each hour of overtime work.

Sometimes a day off **doesn't mean** free time. Many people **don't relax** on their days off. Some people get part-time jobs on these days. High school and college students often have part-time jobs.

Today, the average American worker **doesn't expect to keep** the same job for a long time. Young people change jobs often. Older people **don't like to change** jobs as often. The typical worker **doesn't stay** at one job for more than five years, but people over sixty stay at their jobs for around ten years.

> **DID YOU KNOW?**
> The federal minimum wage is $7.25 per hour. But in some states and cities, the minimum wage is more than $10 per hour.

Vocabulary	Context
job/work	I like my **job**. The **work** is interesting.
make money	She **makes** a lot of **money**. She **makes** $75,000 a year.
wage	My **wages** are $8 an hour.
salary	His **salary** is $40,000 a year.
get paid	I **get paid** on Friday. I take my check to the bank.
day off	Tuesday is my **day off**. I don't work on Tuesdays.
full-time	Simon has a **full-time** job. He works forty hours a week.
complain	She doesn't like her job. She **complains** about it a lot.
extra/overtime	For **extra** work, I get **extra** pay. I like to work **overtime**.
mean	*Weekend* **means** Saturday and Sunday.
relax	We **relax** on Sundays. We don't work. We go to the park.
part-time	Tina has a **part-time** job. She works after school.
average	The **average** American worker changes jobs often.
expect	He **expects** to keep his job for five years.
keep	I have a good job. I want to **keep** my job for a long time.

3

GRAMMAR

The Simple Present—
Yes/No Questions

CONTEXT

Eating Customs

A customer buys food from a food truck in New York City, New York.

BEFORE YOU READ

Circle *yes* or *no*.

1. I like American food.   Yes   No

2. I eat in restaurants often.   Yes   No

READ

Read the following conversation. Pay special attention to *yes/no* questions in the simple present in bold.

Simon and Peter are at a restaurant.

Peter: It's 1:30. It's early. **Do** Americans usually **have** lunch at this time?

Simon: One-thirty is late. Americans usually eat lunch around noon. Some have an hour for lunch and others have thirty minutes. **Do** you **want** to order a sandwich?

Peter: Yes, I do. I'm hungry. Look. That man has a very big salad.

Simon: Yes, some people eat a salad for lunch.

Peter: **Do** people **eat** salads instead of sandwiches?

Simon: Yes, sometimes. Or they have a small sandwich with a small salad or cup of soup.

Peter: **Do** Americans often **eat** in restaurants?

Simon: Yes, they do. They're very busy. They don't always have time to cook every meal. Sometimes they go out to restaurants. Sometimes they order their food from restaurants.

Peter: **Do** restaurants **deliver** food to your home?

Simon: Yes, some do. And many restaurants have *takeout* food. They prepare the food for you. You take it home to eat. Supermarkets sell prepared food too. Usually it's in the deli section. They have hot and cold food. Some supermarkets have tables, and people eat there. But most people take the prepared meals home. Prepared food is very popular because you don't have to cook.

Peter: **Does** prepared food **cost** more?

Simon: Yes, it does. But it's very convenient.

DID YOU KNOW?

58% of Americans eat at a restaurant at least once a week. 14% eat out two or three times a week and 4% eat out more than three times a week.

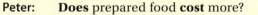

Vocabulary	Context
order	Peter wants to **order** a sandwich. He asks the waiter for a tuna sandwich.
hungry	He's **hungry**. He wants to eat.
meal	I eat three **meals** a day. They are breakfast, lunch, and dinner.
deliver	That restaurant **delivers** pizza. Someone brings it to your house.
takeout	Let's order **takeout**. We can take the food home to eat.
prepared food	**Prepared food** is very popular. It's ready to eat.
deli	Let's go to the **deli** section. They have sandwiches there.
convenient	Prepared food is **convenient**. It's fast and easy.

LISTEN

CD 1
TR 34

Listen to the sentences about the conversation. Circle *true* or *false*.

1. (True)   False   5. True   False

2. True   False   6. True   False

3. True   False   7. True   False

4. True   False   8. True   False

4.8 The Simple Present—*Yes/No* Questions

Do	Subject	Verb (Base Form)		Short Answer
Do	you	**like**	American food?	Yes, I do.
Does	Peter	**go**	to a restaurant for lunch?	Yes, he does.
Does	Simon	**eat**	lunch at 2 p.m.?	No, he doesn't.
Does	this restaurant	**have**	takeout food?	Yes, it does.
Do	the Japanese	**eat**	a lot of cheese?	No, they don't.
Do	we	**have**	time to cook?	No, we don't.
Do	they	**enjoy**	salad?	Yes, they do.

EXERCISE 1 Fill in the blanks with *do* or *does*. Then write a short answer to each question based on the conversation on page 81.

1. ____Does____ the man in the restaurant have a salad? _Yes, he does._____
   a.   b.

2. _____ a sandwich have bread? _____
   a.   b.

3. _____ Peter want to order a salad for lunch? _____
   a.   b.

4. _____ many Americans eat lunch in restaurants? _____
   a.   b.

5. _____ American workers have two hours for lunch? _____
   a.   b.

6. _____ some restaurants deliver to your home? _____
   a.   b.

7. _____ the deli section have hot and cold food? _____
   a.   b.

8. _____ supermarkets often have prepared food? _____
   a.   b.

EXERCISE 2 Complete the conversation between Victor and Simon with the correct question from the box.

Do you work Monday through Friday?	Do you deliver the pizzas? ✓
Does Joe's Pizza have vegetarian pizza?	Does the job pay well?
Do you like your new job?	Do you use your car?

Victor: I have a new part-time job. I work for Joe's Pizza.

Simon: _Do you deliver the pizzas?_ _____
                                        1.

Victor: Yes, I do. I deliver them all over the city.

Simon: _____
                    2.

Victor: No, I don't. I work on the weekends.

Simon: _____
                    3.

Victor: No, I use the restaurant's car. It has a "Joe's Pizza" sign.

Simon: _____
                    4.

Victor: No, it doesn't. But people often give me extra money for the delivery.

We call that money a *tip*.

Simon: _____
                    5.

Victor: Yes, It does. Many people order a pizza with no meat.

Simon: _____
                    6.

Victor: Yes, I do! It's a great job.

EXERCISE 3 Complete each short conversation with a *yes/no* question in the simple present. Use the words given.

1. **A:** Many Americans eat lunch outside the home.

   B: _Do they eat lunch in restaurants?_ _____
                                              eat in restaurants

continued

4

GRAMMAR

The Simple Present—
Wh- Questions

The Simple Present—
Subject Questions

CONTEXT

Exercise

Two thousand people practice yoga at Red Rocks
Amphitheatre, Morrison, Colorado.

BEFORE YOU READ

1. Do you exercise every day?

2. What kind of exercise do you do?

READ

CD 1
TR 36

Read the following conversation. Pay special attention to *wh-* questions in the simple present in bold.

Dorota and Halina are on a walk.

Halina: Look at that woman in a business suit. **Why does** she **have** sneakers on?

Dorota: That's Louisa. She walks during her lunch hour. She wears sneakers on her walks. Some Americans exercise during their lunch hour.

Halina: **Where does** she **walk** in the winter?

Dorota: Maybe she goes to a gym nearby. There are many gyms in the city. Or maybe she goes to a gym in her office.

Halina: In her office? **What do** you **mean**?

Dorota: Some office buildings have gyms for their workers. They're free.

Halina: That's very interesting. I see a lot of people on bicycles here too. Look! **Who rides** a bicycle in traffic downtown?

Dorota: She's a bike messenger. She works on her bicycle. She rides her bike and takes mail from one office to another in the city. Bike messengers always ride fast. They get a lot of exercise every day!

Halina: Do all Americans exercise every day?

Dorota: Some Americans don't exercise at all. They have desk jobs. They sit all day. But many people try to exercise a little every day. I do too.

Halina: **What kind of exercise do** you **do**?

Dorota: I walk. It's great exercise. I stay healthy this way.

Halina: **Where do** you **walk**? In a gym?

Dorota: No. A gym costs money. I go to a park near my house.

Halina: **How often do** you **exercise**?

Dorota: I try to walk five days a week. But I don't always have time.

> ## DID YOU **KNOW?**
> Walk quickly for thirty minutes a day. It is good for your health!

Vocabulary	Context
business suit	A **suit** is a kind of formal clothing. For some jobs, people wear **business suits** to work.
sneakers	I wear **sneakers** when I exercise. They are comfortable.
during	She often walks **during** her lunch hour.
wear	I **wear** a t-shirt in the summer. I **wear** a jacket in the winter.
exercise (n.) exercise (v.)	Louisa walks for **exercise**. Some Americans don't **exercise** a lot.
gym	I go to a **gym**. I exercise there.
nearby	My office is **nearby**. It is very close.
messenger	A **messenger** takes information from place to place.
ride a bicycle/bike	I **ride** my **bicycle** (**bike**) to work.
at all	My father has no vacation time. He doesn't travel **at all**.
desk job	He has a **desk job**. He works at a desk all day.
stay healthy	Dorota exercises a lot and eats well. She **stays healthy** that way.
cost	The gym is expensive. It **costs** a lot of money each month.

LISTEN

Listen to the sentences about the conversation. Circle *true* or *false*.

CD 1
TR 37

1. True   (False)   5. True   False

2. True   False   6. True   False

3. True   False   7. True   False

4. True   False   8. True   False

A bike messenger
in traffic

4.9 The Simple Present—*Wh-* Questions

Question Word(s)	Do	Subject	Verb (Base Form)		Answer
How much	**do**	I	**owe**	you?	Five dollars.
How often	**do**	you	**ride**	your bike?	Three times a week.
Who	**do**	you	**see**	at the gym?	All my friends.
What kind of exercise	**does**	Marta	**do**	normally?	She rides a bike.
What	**does**	"bike"	**mean?**		It means bicycle.
How much	**does**	that bike	**cost?**		It costs about $200.
How many days	**does**	Dorota	**exercise**	outside?	Five days a week.
Why	**do**	we	**exercise?**		Because we want to stay healthy.
Where	**do**	they	**work?**		Near the gym.
When	**do**	Simon and Marta	**walk?**		In the morning.
What	**do**	they	**do**	for exercise?	They walk.

Language Notes:

1. When we ask *how often,* we want to know a number of times.

2. We use *because* with answers to *why* questions.

PART B Compare statements and *wh-* questions.

Statements	Wh- Questions
Marta **rides** her bike.	How often **does** Marta **ride** her bike?
You **walk** fast.	Why **do** you **walk** fast?

EXERCISE 1 Fill in the correct question word in each short conversation. Use *what, who, when, where, how, why, what kind(s) of, how many, how much,* or *how often.* The underlined words are the answers to the questions.

1. **A:** _____How often_____ does she ride her bike?

   B: She rides her bike <u>every day</u>.

2. **A:** _____ does *healthy* mean?

   B: It means <u>not sick</u>.

3. **A:** _____ do they walk every day?

   B: <u>Because it's good exercise</u>.

continued

4. A: _____ hours do they walk every day?

B: They walk <u>for one hour</u> every day.

5. A: _____ shoes does Louisa have?

B: She has <u>sneakers</u>.

6. A: _____ do good sneakers cost?

B: They cost <u>about $100</u>.

7. A: _____ do some people get to work?

B: <u>They ride their bicycles</u>.

8. A: _____ does Dorota walk in the park?

B: She tries to walk <u>five days a week</u>.

9. A: _____ does Louisa exercise?

B: She exercises <u>during her lunch hour</u>.

EXERCISE 2 Write questions with the words given. Write an answer to each question. Use the ideas from the conversation on page 87.

1. what / Halina / ask Dorota

   A: _What does Halina ask Dorota?_

   B: _She asks Dorota about exercise in the United States._

2. what kind of exercise / Dorota / do

   A: _____

   B: _____

3. where / Dorota / exercise

   A: _____

   B: _____

4. when / Louisa / exercise

   A: _____

   B: _____

5. how often / Dorota / exercise

A: _____

B: _____

6. why / people / need to exercise

A: _____

B: _____

7. what / "bike" / mean

A: _____

B: _____

EXERCISE 3 Complete the question in each short conversation.

1. A: Dorota walks for exercise.

   B: How often *does she walk?* _____

2. A: She wears sneakers to work.

   B: Why _____

3. A: Lisa has a day off each week.

   B: When _____

4. A: I have some new shoes.

   B: What kind of _____

5. A: She goes to the gym in the winter.

   B: How often _____

6. A: Peter sees some bikes in the street.

   B: How many _____

7. A: Bike messengers ride fast.

   B: Why _____

8. A: Shafia and Ali like to run.

   B: Where _____

4.10 The Simple Present—Subject Questions

We do not use *do/does* when the question word is the subject.

Question Word(s)	Verb (Base Form or -s Form)		Short Answer
Who	**wants**	a new bike?	Tina does.
Who	**works**	in that company?	We do.
What kind of people	**exercise**	here?	Office workers do.
Which company	**has**	a gym for workers?	My company does.
How many people	**wear**	sneakers to exercise?	Everybody does.
Whose friend	**exercises**	at lunch time?	Dorota's friend does.
What	**happens**	at the gym?	People exercise.

Language Notes:

1. *Who* questions are singular. Answers can be singular or plural.

2. *What kind of* can be plural:

   A: What kinds of events happen in the park?

   B: Free concerts and farmer's markets.

3. *How many* questions are plural. Answers can be singular or plural.

EXERCISE 4 Write a question about each statement. Use the question words given as subjects.

1. Somebody needs a job.

   <u>Who needs a job?</u>
   who

2. Somebody wants to exercise.

   _____
   who

3. Some jobs pay well.

   _____
   what kinds of

4. Some people ride their bicycles to work.

   _____
   how many

5. Some people work three days a week.

   _____
   who

6. Some workers exercise during their lunch hours.

   _____
   which

7. Some people in my company exercise before work.

_____
how many

8. Someone's company has a gym for the workers.

_____
whose

9. Something happens after lunch.

_____
what

EXERCISE 5 Write a *wh-* or subject question to complete each short conversation below. The underlined words are the answers. Some questions may vary.

1. A: What kind of clothes do people wear at the gym?

    B: People wear <u>workout clothes</u> at the gym.

2. A: _____

    B: <u>Because they want to stay healthy</u>.

3. A: _____

    B: <u>Dorota's</u> friend does.

4. A: _____

    B: Some office workers exercise <u>after work in the evening</u>.

5. A: _____

    B: A bike messenger <u>takes mail from one office to another</u>.

6. A: _____

    B: <u>That bike costs over $500</u>.

7. A: _____

    B: Louisa exercises <u>five days a week</u>.

8. A: _____

    B: <u>A bike messenger</u> works on a bicycle.

9. A: _____

    B: Halina and Dorota see <u>only one</u> bike messenger.

WRITING

PART 1 Editing Advice

1. Use the -s form in the affirmative with *he, she, it,* and singular subjects.

   works
   Dorota ~~work~~ in an office.

   has
   She ~~have~~ a good job.

2. Don't use the -s form after *does* or *doesn't.*

   have
   She doesn't ~~has~~ a new job.

   work
   Where does she ~~works~~?

3. Don't use *do* or *does* in questions about the subject.

   wants
   Who ~~does want~~ to go to the gym?

4. Use the correct word order in questions.

   Where does work your friend?

5. Use the correct question word order with *mean* and *cost.*

   does "bike" mean
   What ~~means "bike"~~?

   does that bike cost
   How much ~~costs that bike~~?

6. Don't separate the subject and verb with time expressions of two or more words.

   He three days a week goes to the gym.

7. Use the correct word order with frequency words.

   He goes always to the gym.

   He usually is tired.

PART 2 Editing Practice

Some of the shaded words and phrases have mistakes. Find the mistakes and correct them. If the shaded words are correct, write C.

Simon: Look at that fast bike messenger.

Victor: What does "bike messenger" mean
        ~~What means "bike messenger"?~~
              1.

Simon: A bike messenger delivers things.
                     C
                     2.

Victor: What does a bike messenger delivers?
                     3.

Simon: A bicycle messenger deliver packages to offices downtown.
                     4.

Victor: Who does work as a bicycle messenger?
         5.

Simon: Usually young, healthy people do this job. But the job is not always safe.
6.

Victor: Not safe? Why? What does happen to them?
7.

Simon: People don't always watch for the messengers. They open sometimes their car doors,
8.

and a messenger hits them. And sometimes bike messengers don't stop at red lights.
9.

They ride always very fast.
10.

Victor: Does a messenger make a lot of money?
11.

Simon: Not a lot. Messengers make between $10 and $20 dollars an hour. And they ride often
12.   13.

thirty to forty miles. More work mean more money. But there is a problem. Now companies
14.

send documents by email. There is less work.

Victor: Do they work in bad weather too?
15.

Simon: Yes. And they don't complain. It's part of their job.
16.

Victor: There is one good thing: they get a lot of exercise. Never they need go to a gym!
17.   18.

PART 3 Write About It

Rewrite the following paragraph about Nina. Change *I* to *Nina* or *she*. Make necessary changes to the verbs.

I live in Chicago. I like the city. Why do I like it? Because it's wonderful in the summer! I

often go to a big park downtown. It has concerts every Thursday evening. I don't pay for these

concerts. They're free. I like to visit Lake Michigan. It has many free beaches. But the water is

often cold. I don't swim in June or July. I swim only in August. I also visit a beautiful park on

the lake. Sometimes I have dinner at a restaurant near the lake. I don't do

that often. It's expensive. I sometimes invite friends to visit me in Chicago.

Nina lives in Chicago....

PART 4 Learner's Log

1. Write one sentence about each of these topics:
   - Free-time activities in the United States
   - Work in the United States
   - Eating customs in the United States
   - Exercise in the United States

2. Write any questions you still have about the topics above.

UNIT

5

Traffic on the Santa Monica Highway, California

DRIVING

> Take the back roads instead of the highways.
>
> — Minnie Pearl

1

GRAMMAR

Modal: *Can*—Affirmative and Negative

Modal: *Should*—Affirmative and Negative

Have To—Affirmative and Negative

CONTEXT

Getting a Driver's License

A bilingual driver's manual

BEFORE YOU READ

Circle *yes* or *no*.

1. Do you know how to drive?   Yes   No

2. Do you have a driver's license from this state?   Yes   No

READ

Read the following conversation. Pay special attention to affirmative and negative forms of *can, should,* and *have to* in bold.

Simon's son, Ed, wants to learn to drive. He is fifteen years old.

Ed: Dad, I want to get my driver's license.

Simon: You **have to get** a learner's permit first.

Ed: How do I get that?

Simon: I **can help** you with the rules. But in this state, drivers under the age of eighteen **have to take** a driver's education class at school. It's the law.

Ed: A class takes a long time. I **can learn** faster with you.

Simon: No, you **can't**. It takes a long time to learn to drive. You **shouldn't be** in a hurry. First, you **have to pass** two tests. One is a vision test and the other is a written test. The written test is about the traffic laws. You **have to study** thirty hours in the classroom.

Ed: And then I **can get** my license.

Simon: No. You **can get** a learner's permit. Then you **have to practice** in the car. In this state, you **have to practice** at least fifty hours, but you **should practice** much more. More practice is more experience. And you **have to wait** three months. Then you **can take** the driving test.

Ed: And I **can get** my license. I **can drive** with my friends.

Simon: Not exactly.

Ed: What do you mean?

Simon: Here, drivers under seventeen **have to drive** with an adult driver at night. The adult **has to** be over twenty-one. You **can have** only one other teenager in the car. And you **can't drive** at night. On Friday and Saturday you **can't drive** at all from 11 p.m. to 6 a.m. Sunday through Thursday, you **can't drive** between 10 p.m. and 6 a.m. It's not safe during those hours.

Ed: I don't like that. Are you sure?

Simon: Yes, I am. These laws are for your safety. This law saves a lot of lives every year. You **can go** online and check the state's traffic laws.

DID YOU **KNOW?**

Car crashes are the number-one cause of death for people aged sixteen to nineteen. Many states have laws to protect younger drivers, although the laws are different in each state.

Vocabulary	Context
learner's permit	A new driver practices with a **learner's permit**.
rule	Teenagers can't drive between 11 p.m. and 6 a.m. That's the **rule**.
under/over	Ed is fifteen years old. He's **under** age sixteen. Tina is seventeen years old. She's **over** age sixteen.
law	You have to stop at all stop signs and red lights. It's the **law**.
take time	It **takes** a long **time** to be a good driver. You must practice a lot.
in a hurry	Ed wants his license now. He's **in a hurry.**
pass a test	When you **pass** the **tests**, you can get your learner's permit.
vision test	A **vision test** checks a person's eyes.
written test	We use pencil and paper for **written tests**.
practice (v.) practice (n.)	Ed's new at driving. He has to **practice**. Ed isn't a good driver yet. He needs a lot of **practice**.
at least	He has to practice **at least** fifty hours. He can practice more than fifty hours.
experience	Simon drives every day. He has a lot of **experience** driving.
adult/teenager	Simon is an **adult**. He is forty years old. Ed is a **teenager**. He is fifteen years old.
safety (n.) save (v.)	The laws are for your **safety**. They keep you safe. Seat belts **save** many lives each year.

LISTEN

Listen to the sentences about the conversation. Circle *true* or *false*.

CD 1
TR 39

1. True   (False)
2. True   False
3. True   False
4. True   False
5. True   False
6. True   False
7. True   False
8. True   False

A teenager
learns to drive.

5.1 Modal: *Can*—Affirmative and Negative

We use *can* to show ability, permission, or possibility.

Subject	Can	Verb (Base Form)	
I She Simon It We You They	can cannot can't	help	him.

Language Notes:

1. We write the negative of *can* as one word: *cannot*. The contraction for *cannot* is *can't*.

2. *Can* doesn't have an *-s* ending.

3. The main verb doesn't have an *-s* ending after the affirmative or negative form of *can*.

4. We often use *can't* with rules or laws.

> You **can't** park at a bus stop. It's against the law.

Pronunciation Note:

In affirmative statements, we usually pronounce *can* /kən/. In negative statements, we pronounce *can't* /kænt/. It is hard to hear the final *t*, so we use the vowel sound and stress to tell the difference between *can* and *can't*. Listen to your teacher pronounce these sentences:

> I *can go*. (accent on *go*)   I *can't* go. (accent on *can't*)

EXERCISE 1 Fill in the blanks with *can* or *can't*. Use the ideas from the conversation on page 99.

1. Ed _____can't_____ drive now.

2. Simon _____ help Ed with the rules.

3. Ed _____ get his driver's license now.

4. People _____ find the laws and safe driving practices on the state website.

5. Ed _____ take the driver's education class now.

6. Simon _____ help Ed practice in the car now.

7. Ed _____ get a learner's permit without a driver's education class.

8. Teenagers under seventeen _____ drive alone at night in Ed's state.

9. Teenagers under seventeen _____ have more than one other teenager in the car.

5.2 Modal: *Should*—Affirmative and Negative

We use *should* when we give advice or make a suggestion.

Subject	*Should*	Verb (Base Form)	
I He She We You They	**should** **should not** **shouldn't**	take	the test today.

EXERCISE 2 Give advice in each conversation. Fill in the blank with *should* or *shouldn't* and the words given.

1. **A:** I have my written test tomorrow.

   B: _____*You should read*_____ the driver's handbook again tonight.

           you/read

2. **A:** My car is dirty.

   B: _____ it today!

           you/wash

3. **A:** Ed wants to learn to drive.

   B: _____ in a hurry.

           he/be

4. **A:** Ed wants to be a safe driver.

   B: _____ a lot with a good driver.

           he/practice

5. **A:** I'm very tired today, and I have driving practice.

   B: _____ today. Wait until tomorrow.

           you/drive

6. **A:** Ed doesn't know the driving laws in his state.

   B: _____ them before the written test.

           he/learn

7. **A:** Many cars are on the roads from 4 to 7 p.m.

   B: _____ during those hours.

           new drivers/drive

8. **A:** I don't have the driver's handbook, and I need to study it tonight.

   B: _____ online. The information

           you/look

   is on the state website. You can download a copy of the

   handbook too.

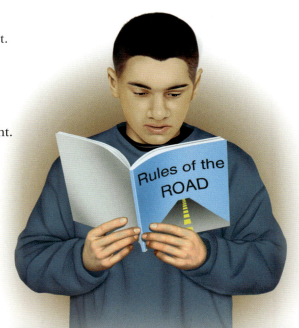

5.3 *Have To*—Affirmative and Negative

Have to shows necessity.

Subject	*Have To*	Verb (Base Form)	
I You We They	**have to** **don't have to**		
		pass	the test now.
She He Ed	**has to** **doesn't have to**		

Language Notes:

1. In the affirmative, *have to* shows laws or strong necessity.

    Ed **has to** get a learner's permit.

2. In the negative, *have to* means not necessary.

    Simon **doesn't have to** work on Saturday.

Pronunciation Note:

In normal speech, we pronounce *have to* /hæftə/. We pronounce *has to* /hæstə/. Listen to your teacher pronounce the following sentences in normal speech:

    We *have to* take the test.   She *has to* drive to work.

EXERCISE 3 Fill in the blanks with the affirmative or negative form of *have to* and the verbs given. Use the ideas from the conversation on page 99.

1. Ed _____ has to take _____ a driver's education class.
       _{take}

2. Simon _____ a learner's permit.
          _{get}

3. All drivers _____ the vision and written tests.
            _{pass}

4. Ed _____ at least fifty hours before the driving test.
       _{practice}

5. People over age eighteen _____ a driver's education class.
                     _{take}

6. Drivers over age eighteen _____ with an adult driver at night.
                      _{be}

7. All drivers _____ a driver's license or permit.
            _{have}

8. Simon _____ Ed the traffic laws. Ed can learn them at school.
          _{teach}

EXERCISE 4 About You Complete the sentences about driving so they are true about your country. Fill in the blanks with the affirmative or negative form of *have to* and the verbs given.

1. We _____ *have to get* _____ a permit before the driving test.
   get

2. We _____ *don't have to finish* _____ high school to get a driver's license.
   finish

3. Drivers _____ eighteen years old to get a driver's license.
   be

4. Drivers under age eighteen _____ a driver's education class.
   take

5. New drivers _____ a vision test.
   pass

6. Young drivers _____ with an adult driver.
   practice

7. New drivers _____ all the answers right on the written test.
   get

8. Young drivers _____ driving at 11 p.m.
   stop

9. New drivers _____ at least three months before the driving test.
   wait

EXERCISE 5 Look at the following road signs from Ed's driver's handbook. Write two sentences about each road sign. Use the affirmative and negative of *can, should,* or *have to*. Answers may vary.

1. Drivers can't go over 65 miles per hour. _____

   Drivers have to go at least 45 miles per hour. _____

2. _____

   _____

3. _____

   _____

4. _____

   _____

5. _____

_____

6. _____

_____

7. _____

_____

8. _____

_____

9. _____

_____

EXERCISE 6 [About You] Complete the sentences about drivers in your country. Answers will vary.

1. They can _learn to drive at age fifteen._ _____

2. They can't _drive without a permit._ _____

3. They can _____

4. They can't _____

5. They should _____

6. They shouldn't _____

7. They have to _____

8. They don't have to _____

EXERCISE 7 Read the following conversations. Fill in the blanks with the affirmative or negative form of *can*, *should*, or *have* to and the verb given. Some answers may vary.

1. **A:** I don't have a car.

    B: Don't worry. You _____ *can use* _____ my car today.

    _{use}

2. **A:** I don't like to drive.

    B: That's OK. You _____ the bus.

    _{take}

3. **A:** Where are your car keys?

    B: They're in the car.

    A: You _____ your keys in the car.

    _{leave}

4. **A:** Today is a holiday. Do you want to go to a movie?

    B: No, I'm sorry. I _____ the traffic laws for my test on Friday.

    _{a. study}

    A: You _____ it today. It's Monday. You have three more days before the test.

    _{b. do}

5. **A:** Your car is very dirty. You _____ it.

    _{a. wash}

    B: I know, but I _____ it today. I'm too busy.

    _{b. wash}

6. **A:** Let's walk to work today.

    B: We don't have time. We _____ at work in thirty minutes.

    _{be}

7. **A:** My son wants to get his driver's license. But he's only fifteen.

    B: Then he _____ a driver's training class first. But don't worry.

    _{a. take}

    He _____ for it. He _____ the class free in school.

    _{b. pay}   _{c. take}

8. **A:** My written test is tomorrow and I don't know the rules of the road.

    B: You _____ to study until the night before the test.

    _{a. wait}

    You _____ all the laws in one night. It's not possible.

    _{b. learn}

9. **A:** There's a good program on TV now about driving safety.

    B: We _____ it.

    _{watch}

    A: Good idea!

CD 1
TR 40

EXERCISE 8 Fill in the blanks in the conversations with the correct verbs from the box.

CONVERSATION A: Ed asks Marta about his friend from Mexico.

doesn't have to get	should study	can drive
has to take	has to get	can use ✓

Ed: Mom, one of my friends has an international driver's license.

He _____*can use*_____ it to drive in this state, right?
       1.

Marta: Yes, he can. But he _____ with an international license for only three months.
                                                    2.

Then he _____ a new driver's license in this state.
                    3.

Ed: What about a learner's permit?

Marta: He _____ a learner's permit. But he _____ the rules of
                        4.   **5.**

the road for this state. Then he _____ all three of the tests. The laws here are
                                                6.

very different from the laws in Mexico.

CONVERSATION B: The driving teacher, Mr. Brown, talks to students in Ed's high school driver's education class.

have to wear	can't see	shouldn't worry

Mr. Brown: Today's class is about the tests for your learner's permit. Does anyone have a question? Karl?

Karl: I'm worried about the vision test. I _____ very well.
                                                              7.

Mr. Brown: You _____ . You can take the test with your glasses on.
                              8.

But then you _____ your glasses in the car too. It's the law.
                          9.

2

Can, Should, and *Have To*—Yes/No Questions

Can, Should, and *Have To*—*Wh-* Questions

Can, Should, and *Have To*—Subject Questions

Car Safety

A father helps his children with their car seats.

BEFORE YOU READ

1. Where should children sit in a car?

2. Do you have a child in your family? If so, what kind of car seat does the child use?

READ

Read the following conversation. Pay special attention to *yes/no* questions and *wh-* questions with *can, should,* and *have to* in bold.

Dorota and Halina are on the way to an outlet mall. Halina asks Dorota about car seats for her daughter, Anna.

Halina: This is my first trip to an outlet mall. **Can** I **get** a new car seat for Anna there? She's too big for her old infant seat now. And she's still too small for a seat belt.

Dorota: Sure. And things aren't so expensive at the outlet mall.

Halina: **What kind** of car seat **should** I **get**?

Dorota: Well, she's two now. Seats for toddlers are different. We can look in several stores.

Halina: **How long does** Anna **have to use** a car seat?

Dorota: In this state, children have to use a car seat until age eight, eighty pounds, or fifty-seven inches tall.

Halina: **Where should** I **put** Anna's seat? **Can** I **put** it on the front passenger seat?

Dorota: No. Anna shouldn't be in the front seat. The air bag can hurt children. They should sit in the back seat until age twelve.

(five minutes later)

Dorota: I have to stop for gas. Here's a gas station.

Halina: I can pay. **Do** we **have to pay** first?

Dorota: Yes, the sign says "Pay First." But don't worry. I can put it on my credit card. I can pay right here at the pump.

Halina: **Should** I **wash** the windows?

Dorota: OK. You can wash the windows. And I can pump the gas.

Halina: **Can** I **buy** water here? I'm thirsty.

Dorota: Yes, you can. This gas station has a store.

DID YOU KNOW?

You can get a ticket if you don't have a child in a car seat. The ticket can be between $10 and $500.

Vocabulary	Context
on the way	They are in the car. They are **on the way** to the mall.
outlet mall	**Outlet malls** have many stores and good prices.
trip	We are in the car. We're on a **trip** out of town.
infant	That baby is only three months old. She's an **infant**.
seat belt	Everyone has to wear a **seat belt** in a car. It keeps you safe.
toddler	A child between the ages of one and three is often called a **toddler**.
several	We can look in **several** stores. I know three good stores.
until	Children sit in the back seat **until** age twelve. Then they can sit in the front seat.
passenger	A **passenger** sits next to the driver or in the back seat.
air bag	In an accident, **air bags** keep the driver and passengers safe.
hurt	An air bag can **hurt** a small child. They can be dangerous.
pump (v.) pump (n.)	We have to **pump** our own gas. We fill the tank. We can pay at the **pump** with a credit card.

LISTEN

 Listen to the sentences about the conversation. Circle *true* or *false*.

CD 1
TR 42

1. (True)   False   5. True   False

2. True   False   6. True   False

3. True   False   7. True   False

4. True   False   8. True   False

5.4 *Can, Should*, and *Have To—Yes/No* Questions

PART A We put *can* or *should* before the subject to make a question.

Modal	Subject	Verb (Base Form)		Short Answer
Can	I	get	some water?	Yes, you can.
Can	young children	sit	in the front seat?	No, they can't.
Should	Halina	buy	an infant seat?	No, she shouldn't.
Should	Halina	get	a new car seat for Anna?	Yes, she should.

PART B We use *do* or *does* to make questions with *have to*.

Do	Subject	Have To	Verb (Base Form)		Short Answer
Does	Dorota	**have to**	get	gas now?	Yes, she does.
Does	a teenager	**have to**	sit	in the back?	No, he/she doesn't.
Do	I	**have to**	pump	the gas?	Yes, you do.
Do	we	**have to**	pay	inside?	No, we don't.

EXERCISE 1 Write a short answer for each question. Use the ideas from the conversation on page 109.

1. Does Dorota have to get gas? <u>Yes, she does.</u>

2. Can Anna sit in the front seat? <u>No, she can't.</u>

3. Should Halina put Anna's car seat in the front passenger seat? _____

4. Can air bags hurt small children? _____

5. Does Dorota have to pay in cash for her gas? _____

6. Can people pump their own gas at the gas station? _____

7. Do children over age eight have to use a car seat? _____

8. Should young children sit in the back seat of the car? _____

9. Do children over age eight have to wear seat belts? _____

EXERCISE 2 Match the parts of the sentences to make *yes/no* questions.

1. Can I pay __c__
2. Can we go _____
3. Should I wash _____
4. Should we buy _____
5. Can I put _____
6. Does Anna have to sit _____
7. Does everyone have to use _____

a. to the outlet mall?
b. a new car?
c. with a credit card? ✓
d. the car seat in the front?
e. in the back seat?
f. the windows for you?
g. a seat belt?

EXERCISE 3 Complete the *yes/no* question with *can, should,* or *have to* and the words given.

1. **A:** It's a beautiful day. _____Can we go_____ for a walk in the park?
   <u>we/go</u>

   B: Yes, we can.

2. **A:** It takes two hours to drive to the mall. _____ gas first?
   <u>we/get</u>

   B: Yes, we do.

3. **A:** Gas in this station is expensive. _____ another station?
   <u>we/try</u>

   B: Yes, we should.

4. **A:** Your car windows are dirty. _____ them for you?
   <u>I/wash</u>

   B: Yes, you can. Thank you.

5. **A:** I have a new car seat for my son. _____ in the back seat?
   <u>he/sit</u>

   B: Yes, he does.

EXERCISE 4 About You Put the words given in the correct order to form a question.
Write a short answer about people and customs in your country. Then share your
answers with a partner.

1. Can people buy food and drinks at gas stations? Yes, they can. _____
   food and drinks/at a gas station/people/can/buy

2. _____
   have to/young children/in a car seat/sit

3. _____
   in the front seat/sit/can/children

4. _____
   pump/their own gas/have to/people

5. _____
   adults/wear/have to/seat belts

5.5 Can, Should, and Have To—Wh- Questions

PART A Can/Should

Question Word(s)	Modal	Subject	Verb (Base Form)		Answer
Where	**can**	Halina	get	a car seat?	At the outlet mall.
How	**can**	parents	keep	their children safe in a car?	They can put them in a car seat.
Why	**should**	we	go	to the outlet mall?	To get a good price.
Which car seat	**should**	I	buy	for Anna?	This one is good.

PART B Have To

Question Word(s)	Do	Subject	Have To	Verb (Base Form)		Answer
Where	**does**	Anna	**have to**	sit?		In the back seat.
How much	**do**	we	**have to**	spend	for a car seat?	Between $60 and $150.

EXERCISE 5 Answer each question. Use the ideas from the conversation on page 109.

1. How can people pay for gas?

   <u>They can pay with a credit card or cash.</u>

2. When can a child sit in the front passenger seat?

   _____

3. Why does a small child have to sit in the back seat?

   _____

4. Where can people pay for gas at the gas station?

   _____

5. Why does Halina have to get a new car seat for Anna?

   _____

6. Where can Halina buy water?

   _____

continued

7. What kind of seat should Halina buy?

   _____

8. Why does Dorota have to stop at a gas station?

   _____

9. How can children ride safely in a car?

   _____

EXERCISE 6 Ask a question about each statement using the question word(s) given.

1. Anna has to sit in the back seat.

   Why _does Anna have to sit in the back seat?_ _____

2. They have to stop for gas on their trip.

   How often _____

3. Everyone should drive carefully.

   Why _____

4. An air bag can hurt small children.

   How _____

5. Halina has to buy some things for Anna.

   What _____

6. Anna can't sit in the front seat right now.

   When _____

7. You should get a new car seat for your daughter.

   Why _____

8. You have to pay a lot for this car seat.

   How much _____

EXERCISE 7 Complete each short conversation with a question. Use the words given.

1. **A:** Please get in the car.

   B: <u>Where should we sit?</u>
   <small>where / we / should sit</small>

2. **A:** There's child safety information online.

   B: _____
   <small>which website / I / should check</small>

3. **A:** Halina doesn't have a good car seat for Anna.

   B: _____
   <small>where / she / can buy a good one</small>

4. **A:** Anna is two years old.

   B: _____
   <small>what kind of car seat / Halina / have to buy for her</small>

5. **A:** Car seats have different prices.

   B: _____
   <small>how much / I / should spend</small>

6. **A:** My son is two years old. Do I need a car seat?

   B: Yes. Toddlers have to sit in car seats

   A: _____
   <small>why they / have to sit in car seats</small>

   B: They can get hurt in an accident.

7. **A:** You should buy a new car seat for your son when he's bigger. He's still very small.

   B: _____
   <small>when / I / should buy a new one</small>

5.6 *Can, Should,* and *Have To*—Subject Questions

PART A *Can/Should*

Question Word(s)	Modal	Verb (Base Form)		Answer
What	**can**	happen	to the baby in the front seat?	The air bag can hurt her.
How many people	**can**	sit	in the back seat?	Three can.
Who	**should**	pay	for the gas?	Dorota should.

PART B *Have To*

Question Word(s)	*Have To*	Verb (Base Form)		Answer
Who	**has to**	stop	for gas?	Dorota does.
Which children	**have to**	sit	in the back seat?	All small children do.

EXERCISE 8 Complete each short conversation with a question. Use the following question words as subjects: *who, which, how many,* or *what*. The underlined words are the answer.

1. **A:** Who has to buy a car seat?

   B: Halina has to buy a car seat.

2. **A:** _____

   B: Amy should use a car seat. It will keep her safe.

3. **A:** _____

   B: The gas station on my street can give us the best price for gas.

4. **A:** _____

   B: Young children should sit in the back seat.

5. **A:** _____

   B: Two people have to travel today.

6. **A:** _____

   B: Air bags can hurt children in a car.

7. **A:** _____

   B: Drivers under age seventeen have to drive with an adult at night.

8. A: _____

   B: <u>Halina</u> should buy some water.

9. A: _____

   B: <u>This car seat</u> is very popular.

EXERCISE 9 Marta and Simon talk about Ed's driving practice. Fill in the blanks in their conversation with a phrase from the box.

CD 1
TR 43

When does he have to take	Can you put	I have to take	Ed should learn
Do you have to use✓	We can stop	He should practice	

Marta: _____ Do you have to use _____ the car today?
                                 1.

Simon: Yes.

Marta: _____ some gas in the car for me? It's almost empty.
                        2.

Simon: Sure. _____ Ed out for driving practice later this afternoon.
                                3.

_____ at the gas station. _____
            4.   5.

how to pump gas too.

Marta: _____ the driving test?
                        6.

Simon: In just three weeks!

Marta: _____ a lot. He doesn't have much time.
                        7.

WRITING

PART 1 Editing Advice

1. Always use the base form after *can*, *should*, and *have to.*

   drive
   She can ~~drives~~ the car.

2. Don't use *to* after *can* and *should.*

   The child can't ~~to~~ sit in the front seat.

3. Use the correct word order in a question.

   Why ⟨you⟩ can't drive?

4. Don't forget to use *do* or *does* with *have to* in questions.

   do
   Why ^ you have to take a vision test?

5. Don't use *do* or *does* with subject questions.

   has
   Who ~~does have~~ to sit in the back? The baby does.

PART 2 Editing Practice

Some of the shaded words and phrases have mistakes. Find the mistakes and correct them.
If the shaded words are correct, write C.

This is a conversation between Ed and his driving teacher after the first class.

Ed:	*do* How many pages ^ we have to study in the driver's handbook for tomorrow? **1.**
Mr. Brown:	*C* You should learn the laws in the first twenty pages. **2.**
Ed	Tell me about licenses in this state. When I can drive with my friends? **3.**
Mr. Brown:	You're only sixteen. In this state, you can to have only one passenger in the car **4.** under age twenty-one. And you still has to have an adult in the car between 10 p.m. **5.** and 6 a.m. for the first six months.
Ed:	How many hours we have to practice before the driving test? **6.**
Mr. Brown:	Sixty hours. But you should to practice more. And you have to practice ten hours at night. **7.**
Ed:	How we can do that? We can't drive at night. **8.** **9.**
Mr. Brown:	Sunday through Thursday, you can drive until 10 p.m. and then an adult driver has to goes with you. **10.**

Ed: Does the adult has to be one of my parents?
                                 11.

Mr. Brown: No, but the adult has to be at least twenty-one years old. And the adult has to have a
                                                                                                              12.

                  valid license.

Ed: Yes, I know. And we have to wear a seat belt too.
                                 13.

PART 3 Write About It

Write about what is wrong in each picture. Write one negative and one affirmative sentence about each picture. Use *can, should,* and *have to.*

A.

B.

C.

D.

A. The baby can't sit on the mother's lap. The baby has to be in an infant seat.

PART 4 Learner's Log

1. Use *can, should,* and *have to* (affirmative and/or negative) to write one sentence about each of these topics. Give advice, rules, or information.
   - Rules about children's car seats
   - Things you can do at a gas station
   - What you need for a driver's license

2. Write any questions you still have about the topics above.

SCHOOL

A girl paints in an art class.

A school is a building of four walls...with tomorrow inside.

— Dan Valentine

1

GRAMMAR

Modal: *Must*—Affirmative and Negative Statements

Must and *Have To*

Must Not and *Don't Have To*

CONTEXT

School Lunch Programs

Children in line for lunch, Hagerstown, Maryland

BEFORE YOU READ

1. Are there guidelines for school lunches in your country?   Yes   No

2. Do elementary schools in your country give free lunches to children?   Yes   No

READD

CD 1
TR 44

READ

Read the following article. Pay special attention to affirmative and negative statements with *must* and *have to* in bold.

Children need good nutrition. The United States has the National School Lunch Program to give children well-balanced meals. Schools in this program **must follow** guidelines. They **must not serve** children a lot of fat, sugar, or salt. They **must serve** food from each of these five groups: protein (for example, meat, fish, or beans), vegetables, fruit, grains and bread, and milk.

Parents **must fill out** an application to get free lunch for their children. They **must tell** the truth about their family income.

Some families don't make much money. These families **have to pay** a small amount (less than fifty cents). Children from very low-income families **don't have to pay** for a school lunch at all. Some families have enough money and **have to pay** the full price. But it isn't expensive. It's usually less than three dollars.

Children **don't have to eat** the school lunch. They can bring a lunch from home.

School lunch of a sandwich, milk, orange slices, potatoes, and cookies

DID YOU KNOW?

In the United States, over 30 million children participate in the National School Lunch Program.

Vocabulary	Context
nutrition	Children need good **nutrition**. They need to eat healthy food, such as fruits and vegetables.
balanced	A **balanced** lunch has items from each food group: protein, fruit, vegetables, grains, and milk.
guideline	The National School Lunch Program makes **guidelines**. They tell the schools what to serve.
serve	Schools give children lunch. They **serve** lunch every day.
fat	French fries and potato chips have a lot of **fat**. They are not good for you.
grain	We use **grains** to make bread.
tell the truth	**Tell the truth** on the application. Don't give false information.
income (n.) low-income (adj.)	Their **income** is $30,000 a year. They are a **low-income** family.
amount	Fifty cents is a small **amount** of money.
less than	The lunch costs $2.25. It's **less than** $3.00.

LISTEN

Listen to the sentences about the article. Circle *true* or *false*.

1. (True) False
2. True False
3. True False
4. True False

5. True False
6. True False
7. True False
8. True False

6.1 Modal: *Must*—Affirmative and Negative Statements

Examples	Explanation
Schools **must** serve milk to children. Parents **must** fill out an application for the free lunch program.	We use *must* to show rules or laws.
School lunches **must not** have a lot of sugar. School lunches **must not** have a lot of fat.	When the rule is "don't do this," we use *must not*.

EXERCISE 1 Fill in the blanks with one of the verbs from the box.

be	fill out	tell	sign	pay ✓	serve

1. The lunch is not free for everyone. Some families must _____pay_____.

2. The school must _____ a nutritious lunch with protein, vegetables, fruit, grains, and milk.

3. Parents must _____ an application for the school lunch program.

4. Parents must _____ the application.

5. Parents must _____ the truth about their family income.

6. School lunches must _____ well-balanced.

EXERCISE 2 Read the application for the school lunch program below. Then change sentences 1-9 from imperative statements to statements with *must* or *must not*.

Application for Free and Reduced Price Meals

To apply for free and reduced price meals for your child(ren), you must fill out this form and sign it. Use a black or blue pen.

PART 1: List the names of children at school.

Name(s) of Child(ren) Last Name, First Name	Age	School	Grade	Class
1.				
2.				
3.				

PART 2: List the names of all adult household members and their monthly incomes.

Last Name, First Name	Monthly Income
1.	
2.	
3.	

PART 3: Signature and Social Security Number. I certify that all the above information is true.

Signature of Parent or Guardian	Mailing Address
Social Security Number	**Phone Number**
– –	( )

FOR SCHOOL USE ONLY   Date Received: _____   Date Approved: _____

1. Print your answers. You must print your answers. _____
2. Don't use a pencil. You must not use a pencil. _____
3. Fill out the application. _____
4. Sign your name. _____
5. Don't print your name in Part 3. _____
6. Don't write in the last box. _____
7. Write your monthly income. _____
8. Don't use a red pen. _____
9. Don't give false information. _____

6.2 Must and Have To

Must and have to have similar meanings.

Examples	Explanation
You **must** write your family income. You **have to** write your family income. Schools **must** serve children milk. Schools **have to** serve children milk.	Must is very formal. We use must for rules and laws. We can also use have to for rules and laws. Must is stronger than have to.
Marta **has to** make lunch for her daughter. We **have to** buy more bread.	We use have to for personal necessity. We don't use must for personal necessity.

Language Note:

Have to is more common than must in questions.

Do I **have to** sign the application?

Do schools **have to** serve milk?

EXERCISE 3 Fill in the blanks with *must* + a verb to talk about rules. Use one of the verbs from the box. Answers will vary.

give	include	apply	state	follow	serve	provide	serve

1. Students _____ must apply _____ for the school lunch program.

2. Schools _____ guidelines from the National School Lunch Program.

3. On an application, parents _____ their names.

4. On the school lunch application, parents _____ their family income.

5. School lunches _____ food from each of the five groups.

6. Schools _____ children milk with every lunch.

EXERCISE 4 About You Fill in the blanks to talk about personal necessities. Use *have to* + a verb.

1. I _____ have to call my mom _____ every day.

2. In class, we _____.

3. The teacher _____.

4. My mother _____.

5. Children _____.

6. My classmates _____.

6.3 *Must Not* and *Don't Have To*

Must and *have to* have similar meanings. *Must not* and *don't have to* have different meanings.

Examples	Explanation
School lunches **must not** have a lot of fat. You must tell the truth. You **must not** give false information.	*Must not* gives a rule.
Children **don't have to** eat the school lunch. They can bring a lunch from home. Children of low-income families **don't have to** pay for lunch. They can get a free lunch.	*Don't have to* shows that something is not necessary.

EXERCISE 5 About You Work with a partner. Name three things you don't have to do on the weekends.

I don't have to work on Saturdays.

EXERCISE 6 About You Work with a partner. Name three things students must not do at this school or in this class.

Students must not talk in the library.

EXERCISE 7 Fill in the blanks with the negative of *must* or *have to*. Remember, they have different meanings.

1. Schools in the lunch program _____ *must not* _____ serve a lot of sugar.

2. Children _____ *don't have to* _____ be in the school lunch program.

3. Many families in the school lunch program _____ pay. Their children get free lunch.

4. Maya _____ eat at school. She can eat at home.

5. Parents _____ give false information on the application. They will get in trouble.

6. You _____ drink the milk. You can drink water.

7. Ed _____ study at home. He can study in the library.

8. You _____ talk loudly in the school library. It's a rule.

9. Children _____ come late to school. Everyone should be on time.

2

GRAMMAR

Count and Noncount Nouns

Quantity Expressions with Noncount Nouns

A Lot Of/Much/A Little with Noncount Nouns

Some/Any with Noncount Nouns

CONTEXT

Favorite Foods for School Lunches

A student visits an apple orchard in Woodstock, Vermont.

BEFORE YOU READ

1. What foods are good for children?

2. What are some foods children don't like to eat?

READ

Read the following blog. Pay special attention to quantity expressions with count and noncount nouns in bold.

It's time for a new school year. Today's topic is school lunches for your kids! Your children have two choices: buy a lunch at school or bring a lunch from home.

School lunches can be inexpensive and convenient. They usually provide **a piece of fruit, a carton of milk**, and a protein, such as **a piece of fish** or **meat**, or maybe **a slice of pizza** or a sandwich. Pizza is always a favorite choice with kids. Unfortunately, kids sometimes throw the fruit away. Sometimes, students want **a bottle of soda** or **a piece of candy**, but these are not healthy choices.

Other students bring their lunches to school. They use a brown bag or a lunch box. Their parents help them pack lunches with sandwiches, fruit, vegetables, and maybe a healthy cookie or snack. Some parents still pack **a bag of chips** or a candy bar. These choices have **a lot of fat** or **sugar**, and aren't very healthy. Vegetables are very healthy and don't have **any sugar**. They don't have **much fat** either. Fruit is also a better choice than a candy bar. **A bunch of grapes** is a perfect snack. If you and your child pack a lunch together, you can choose healthy options that he or she wants to eat.

DID YOU KNOW?

The U.S. government's *Smart Snacks in School* nutrition standards limit the calories, sodium, fat, and sugar in all foods and drinks sold at schools.

Vocabulary	Context
favorite	Maya loves pizza. Pizza is her **favorite** lunch.
unfortunately	We use **unfortunately** to introduce bad news.
throw away	Please **throw away** your lunch bag after you eat. Don't leave it on the table.
brown bag (n.)	A **brown bag** is a paper bag for lunches. You can carry your lunch in a **brown bag**.
lunch box	Some kids take their lunches to school in a **lunch box**.
better	Juice is good, but water is **better**.
bunch of	The kids sometimes get a small **bunch of** grapes with lunch.
option	Fruit is a better **option** than candy.

Lesson 2   Favorite Foods for School Lunches   **129**

3

GRAMMAR

Some vs. *Any*

A Lot Of and *Many* vs. *Much*

A Few vs. *A Little*

How Many vs. *How Much*

CONTEXT

School Supplies

A student with his school supplies

BEFORE YOU READ

1. What do children need for school?

2. Should children wear uniforms?

READ

CD 1
TR 50

Read the following conversation. Pay special attention to quantity expressions with count and noncount nouns in bold.

It's Maya's first day of school. She has a note for Victor.

Victor: What's this?

Maya: It's a note from school. It has **a lot of information** and a list of school supplies. I need **a lot of supplies**.

Victor: What do you need?

Maya: I need two erasers, one ruler, two spiral notebooks, ten pencils, one glue stick, one pair of scissors, one package of notebook paper, four folders, one box of tissues, and crayons.

Victor: **How many crayons** do you need?

Maya: One box of twenty-four.

spiral notebook
notebook paper
glue stick
crayons
folders
ruler
scissors
eraser
tissues

Victor calls Simon for help.

Victor: I have **a few questions** about my daughter's school. I need **some advice**. Do you have **any time** now?

Simon: Yes, Victor. I have **a little time** now.

Victor: Oh thank you, Simon! Maya has a list of school supplies. Where can I buy them?

Simon: **Many stores** sell school supplies, but the office supply store near my house has a sale now. I have **a few coupons**. We can go together.

Victor: Do I have to buy **any books**? **How much money** do I need for books?

Simon: You don't have to buy **any books**. Public schools supply the books. Students return them at the end of the school year.

Victor: That's good. The note has **a lot of information** about homework. Do American kids get **a lot of homework**?

Simon: Yes, they do.

Victor: One more question. Do I have to buy a uniform for my daughter?

Simon: I don't know. Children in some schools need uniforms. Let me read the information from Maya's school.

DID YOU KNOW?
On average, a family spends $100 on school supplies per child every year.

Vocabulary	Context
note	The teacher sometimes writes a **note** to parents.
supplies (n.) supply (v.)	Children need school **supplies**. They need pencils, paper, rulers, and more. The school **supplies** students with books. The students use the school's books.
advice	Victor needs Simon's **advice** about school.
coupon	I like to save money. I can get fifty cents off with this **coupon** from the newspaper.
public school	Every child can go to **public school**. Public school is free.
return	Students don't keep the school's books. They **return** them to the school.
uniform	In some schools, all the children wear the same outfit, or clothing. This is a **uniform**.

LISTEN

CD 1
TR 51

Listen to the sentences about the conversation. Circle *true* or *false*.

1. (True)   False   5. True   False

2. True   False   6. True   False

3. True   False   7. True   False

4. True   False   8. True   False

6.8 *Some* vs. *Any*

Examples	Explanation
Maya has **some** information from her teacher. Victor has **some** questions for Simon.	We use *some* with noncount nouns and plural count nouns.
Does she need **any/some** glue? Does she need **any/some** pencils?	We use *any* or *some* with both noncount nouns and plural count nouns in questions.
Maya doesn't have **any** homework today. Victor doesn't have **any** coupons.	We use *any* with both noncount nouns and plural count nouns in negatives.

Language Note:

Homework, information, and *advice* are noncount nouns. They have no plural form. To add a specific quantity, we can say *a homework assignment, a piece of information, a piece of advice.*

EXERCISE 1 Fill in the blanks with *some* or *any*.

1. I need ___*some*___ paper for school.

2. Do you have _____ homework today?

3. We have _____ math homework.

4. I don't have _____ problems with my homework.

5. Maya needs _____ notebooks.

6. I don't need _____ paper for my gym class.

7. Do you need _____ erasers for school?

8. We need _____ crayons for school.

9. Victor needs _____ advice from Simon.

10. Does the school offer _____ after-school programs?

EXERCISE 2 About You Answer the questions. Use *some* or *any* in your answers.

1. Do you have any time to watch TV?

   Yes. I have some time to watch TV after school.

2. Do you have any homework today?

   _____

3. Do you need any books for this course?

   _____

4. Does this class have any students from Korea?

   _____

5. Do you need any paper to do this exercise?

   _____

6. Do you have any information about universities in the United States?

   _____

7. Do you have any advice for new students?

   _____

continued

6.11 How Many vs. How Much

Examples	Explanation
How many coupons do you have? **How many** pencils does Maya need for school?	We use *how many* with count nouns.
How much paper does she need? **How much** money do I need for books?	We use *how much* with noncount nouns.
How much does this book cost? **How much** is the school lunch?	We use *how much* to ask about cost.

EXERCISE 6 About You Find a partner. Ask these questions about elementary schools in your partner's country. Write short answers.

1. How many days a week do kids go to school? <u>five days a week</u>

2. How many months a year do kids go to school? _____

3. How many kids are in an average class? _____

4. How much time do kids spend on homework? _____

5. How many hours a day are kids in school? _____

6. How much time do kids have for vacation? _____

7. How much money do kids spend on books? _____

8. Do kids get school lunch? How much does it cost? _____

9. Do kids wear a uniform? How much does a uniform cost? _____

EXERCISE 7 About You Fill in the blanks with *how much* or *how many*. Then answer the question.

1. <u>How many</u> lessons do we do a day? <u>We do one lesson a day.</u>
   a.   b.

2. _____ classes do you have now? _____
   a.   b.

3. _____ money do you need to take one class? _____
   a.   b.

4. _____ paper do you need for your homework? _____
   a.   b.

5. _____ students in this class speak Spanish? _____
   a.   b.

6. _____ books do we need for this course? _____
   a.   b.

7. _____ time do you spend on your homework? _____
   a.   b.

8. _____ homework do you have today? _____
   a.   b.

🎧 CD 1 TR 52 **EXERCISE 8** Circle the correct word(s) to complete this conversation between a parent, Mrs. Gomez, and a school employee, Mr. Johnson.

Mrs. Gomez: I have (*a little* / *a few*) questions. I need (*a little* / *a few*) information.
1.   2.

Do you have (*any* / *many*) time to answer my questions?
3.

Mr. Johnson: Yes. I have (*a little* / *a few*) time right now.
4.

Mrs. Gomez: Can my kids get into the free lunch program?

Mr. Johnson: It depends on your income. If you don't make (*many* / *much*) money, they can probably
5.

get into the free lunch program.

Mrs. Gomez: I don't make (*many* / *a lot of*) money. What should I do?
6.

Mr. Johnson: You have to fill out a form. The form has (*many* / *much*) questions.
7.

Mrs. Gomez: (*How much* / *How many*) does a school lunch cost?
8.

Mr. Johnson: In this city, the full price is $2.25. That's not (*much* / *any*) money for a healthy lunch.
9.

Mrs. Gomez: I have (*a lot of* / *much*) kids in school, so for me it's (*much* / *a lot of*) money.
10.   11.

Mr. Johnson: (*How much* / *How many*) kids do you have?
12.

Mrs. Gomez: Six. Four are in school, so I really need to learn about the free lunch program.

Mr. Johnson: Let me get you the form.

A school employee helps a parent with paperwork.

WRITING

PART 1 Editing Advice

1. Don't use *to* after *must*.

   have to/must
   Schools ~~must to~~ serve a healthy lunch.

2. Don't put *a* or *an* before a noncount noun.

   I like to eat ~~a~~ rice.

3. Use *of* with a unit of measure.

   of
   I want a cup ˄coffee.

4. Don't forget *of* with *a lot of*.

   of
   I don't have a lot ˄homework today.

5. Don't confuse *much* and *many*, *a little* and *a few*.

   many
   He doesn't have ~~much~~ friends.

   much
   Maya doesn't have ~~many~~ homework today.

   few
   I eat a ~~little~~ grapes every day.

   little
   Put a ~~few~~ salt in the soup.

6. Don't use *much* in affirmative statements.

   a lot of
   He drinks ~~much~~ tea.

7. Don't use *no* after a negative verb.

   any
   I don't have ~~no~~ money.

8. Don't use the plural form with noncount nouns.

   information
   Victor gets a lot of ~~informations~~ from Simon.

PART 2 Editing Practice

Some of the shaded words and phrases have mistakes. Find the mistakes and correct them. If the shaded words are correct, write *C*.

Maya is home with Victor after school.

Maya: Can I have ~~a little~~ grapes? And can I have some milk too?
a few — 1.   C — 2.

Victor: I'm sorry. We don't have no milk today. Do you want a glass water?
3.   4.

Maya: I don't like to drink a water. Do we have any juice?
5.   6.

Victor: Yes, but you can have just a little. Juice contains much sugar.
7.   8.

| Maya: | Soda contains a lot sugar. |
| | 9. |

| Victor: | That's why we don't drink any soda. It's not very healthy. |
| | 10. |

| Maya: | Oh. Can I watch TV now? |

| Victor: | Do you have any homework today? Do your homework first please. Then you can watch TV. |
| | 11. |

| Maya: | Ok. I just have a homework for math. And I have a form for a school trip. You must to sign it. |
| | 12. | 13. |

| Victor: | I have to read it first. Hmmm. I don't understand something here. |
| | 14. |

I have to call Simon for some advices.
15.

PART 3 Write About It

1. Use information from Exercise 6 on page 142 to write a short paragraph of five or six sentences about schools in your partner's country.

Akio is from Japan. In Japan, kids go to school five days a week…

2. Rewrite the following paragraph. Add a quantity word or expression before the underlined words.

I buy healthy food for my family. And I try to be a good example for my family. Here are examples. I drink water before each meal. Then I'm not so hungry. I don't drink soda. Sometimes I drink tea after a meal. I have cereal or eggs for breakfast. I have salad with soup for lunch. I eat fruit every day too. I don't eat red meat. I try to eat fish or chicken every week. I also try to eat beans for protein. I always eat vegetables with dinner. Friends ask me about food for their kids. I always give them advice: "A parent has to be a good example."

I buy a lot of healthy food for my family…

PART 4 Learner's Log

1. Write one sentence about each of these topics:
   - Rules for school lunch programs
   - Foods in school lunch programs
   - Healthy foods
   - School supplies

2. Write any questions you still have about the topics above.

SHOPPING

People buy vegetables at Pike Place
Market in Seattle, Washington.

About eighty percent of the food on shelves of supermarkets today didn't exist 100 years ago.

—Dr. Larry McCleary, author of the book
Feed Your Brain, Lose Your Belly

1

GRAMMAR

Time Expressions with Prepositions

Time Expressions without Prepositions

Prepositions of Place

Prepositions in Common Expressions

CONTEXT

Buying Necessary Things

A man enters a small market at night.

BEFORE YOU READ

1. What stores do you like? Why?

2. Do you shop late at night? Why or why not?

READ

CD 2
TR 2

Read the following conversation between Sue and Rick, an American couple. Pay special attention to the prepositions and expressions in bold.

Rick and Sue are at their home.

Sue: Look. We're **out of** coffee. We need coffee for tomorrow morning. Can you go out and buy some?

Rick: Now? It's late. It's **after** 9:30. We can get it **in** the morning. I always wake up early. I can go shopping **before** breakfast.

Sue: Tomorrow is Saturday. The store is always crowded **on** Saturdays. I don't like to shop **on** the weekend. Anyway, we like to drink coffee **in** the morning.

Rick: But the supermarket is closed **at** night.

Sue: You're right. But the convenience store is open. It's open **24/7**.

Rick: My news program is **on** TV **at** 10 p.m. I don't have time **before** the news. It starts **in** 20 minutes.

Sue: You can go **after** the news.

Rick is now at the convenience store. Sue calls him on his cell phone.

Rick: Hello?

Sue: Hi. Are you **at** the convenience store now?

Rick: I'm still **in** the car. I'm **in** the parking lot.

Sue: Can you go **to** the pharmacy too and get some aspirin? I have a headache.

Rick: Can I get the aspirin **at** the convenience store?

Sue: You can, but aspirin is **on** sale this week **at** the pharmacy—two bottles **for** $7.00. It costs $7.00 **for** one bottle **at** the convenience store.

Rick: Which pharmacy?

Sue: The pharmacy **near** the convenience store. It's **on** the corner. It's **next to** the gas station.

Rick: Is the pharmacy open late too?

Sue: Yes, it's open **24/7**.

DID YOU KNOW?
Prices at a convenience store are sometimes high. You are paying for the convenience of a store that is open 24 hours a day, seven days a week (24/7).

Vocabulary	Context
wake up	Rick **wakes up** early. He has to go to work.
go shopping shop	I like to **go shopping** early. There aren't many other customers at the stores. I like to **shop** at night.
convenience store	A **convenience store** is a small supermarket. It's open late, often 24/7.
program	TV has many **programs**. Every hour you can see a different show.
news	The **news** tells us about local, national, and international events.
still	Rick's not at the store yet. He's **still** in his car.
aspirin	My back hurts sometimes. Then I take **aspirin** to feel better.
headache	My head hurts. I have a terrible **headache**.
pharmacy	You can buy aspirin and other medicine in a **pharmacy**.
corner	The store is on the **corner** of Main Street and Willow Street.

LISTEN

Listen to the sentences about the conversation. Circle *true* or *false*.

CD 2
TR 3

1. (True)   False
2. True   False
3. True   False

4. True   False
5. True   False
6. True   False

7. True   False
8. True   False

7.1 Time Expressions with Prepositions

Prepositions are connecting words. We can use prepositions with time expressions.

The store is open	**in** the morning.
	in the daytime.
	in the afternoon.
	in the evening.
	at night.
The news program starts	**at** 10 p.m.
	in 20 minutes.
You can go out	**after** 9:30.
	after the news program.
	after work.
Sue goes to sleep	**before** 10:30.
The stores are crowded	**on** Saturdays.
	on the weekend.

Language Note:

A sentence can have two time expressions.

> Rick goes to work **at** 7 **in** the morning.

> He wakes up **at 8** a.m. **on** the weekend.

EXERCISE 1 Fill in the blanks with the correct preposition of time: *in, on, after, before,* or *at.*

1. Sue and Rick don't work _____at_____ night.

2. They work _____ Mondays.

3. Lisa doesn't work _____ the evening.

4. Simon doesn't work _____ the weekend.

5. They can buy coffee _____ the morning.

6. Many stores open _____ 9 a.m.

7. The convenience store is open _____ night.

8. It's 5:37 now. It's _____ 5:30.

9. We go shopping _____ the afternoon.

10. The supermarket closes at 10 p.m. Go there _____ 10.

EXERCISE 2 About You Work with a partner. Ask a question with *when do you* and the words given. Your partner will answer.

1. watch TV

   A: When do you watch TV?

   B: I watch TV at night.

2. drink coffee

3. relax

4. go to sleep

5. wake up

6. go shopping

7. listen to OR watch the news

8. wash your clothes

9. eat lunch

10. read blogs

11. see your friends

12. do your homework

13. take an aspirin

14. work

7.2 Time Expressions without Prepositions

In some cases, we don't use a preposition with a time expression.

The store is open	**24 hours a day**.
	seven days a week.
We shop	**three times a month**.
They buy milk	**once a week**.
We cook	**every day**.
The convenience store is open	**24/7**.
	all day and all night.

EXERCISE 3 About You Fill in the blanks. Share your answers with a partner.

1. I ___visit my parents___ once a month.

2. I _____ five days a week.

3. I _____ twice a day.

4 I _____ four times a month.

5. I _____ all day.

6. I _____ every day.

EXERCISE 4 About You Fill in the blanks with a time expression. Tell about the people and places in your country. Share your answers with a partner.

1. People usually watch the news _____ _every day_ _____.

2. Most people use the Internet _____.

3. Pharmacies are usually open _____.

4. Supermarkets in big cities are open _____.

5. Convenience stores are open _____.

6. Most banks are open _____.

7. Most people shop for food _____.

8. Students go to school _____.

EXERCISE 5 About You Ask a question with *how many* and the words given. Another student will answer.

1. days a week/work

    A: How many days a week do you work?

    B: I work five days a week.

2. hours a day/talk on the phone

3. hours a day/spend online

4. times a month/go to the library

5. hours a night/sleep

6. times a day/cook

7. days a week/shop for food

8. minutes a day/exercise

7.3 Prepositions of Place

We can use prepositions with a place.

Preposition	Examples
in	Rick is **in** the car.
	He is **in** the parking lot.
near	The pharmacy is **near** the convenience store.
next to	The pharmacy is **next to** the gas station.
on	The convenience store is **on** the corner.
at	Rick is **at** the convenience store now.
	Sue and Rick are **at** home in the evening.
	They are **at** work in the daytime.
to	Go **to** the pharmacy.

Language Note:

Compare the following sentences:

I'm **in** the store. (I'm not outside the store.)

I'm **at** the store. (I may be inside or in the parking lot, ready to go in.)

EXERCISE 6 Victor and Lisa are on the telephone. Lisa is at home. Victor is about to go into class. He is on his cell phone. Fill in the blanks with the correct preposition: *in, on, at, to, near,* or *next to.*

Victor: Hello?

Lisa: Hi, Victor. Where are you now?

Victor: I'm ____*at*____ school.
1.

Where are you?

Lisa: I'm _____ home. Are you _____ class?
2. **3.**

Victor: No, I'm _____ the parking lot. My class starts in ten minutes.
4.

Lisa: Can you go _____ the store on your way home? We need milk. There's a sale _____
5. **6.**

Tom's Market.

Victor: Where's Tom's Market?

Lisa: It's _____ the school. It's not far. It's _____ the corner. It's _____ the laundromat.
7. **8.** **9.**

Victor: My class is over _____ 9. Is the market still open at 9?
10.

Lisa: Yes, it is. It closes at 9:30. Go _____ the store right away, please.
11.

7.4 Prepositions in Common Expressions

We can use prepositions in many common expressions.

Preposition	Examples
on	Rick is **on the phone**.
	The news program is **on TV**.
	You can hear the news **on the radio**.
	Aspirin is **on sale**.
	Please buy some milk **on your way** home.
for	Aspirin is on sale this week, two bottles **for $7.00**.
out of	We don't have any coffee. We're **out of** coffee.

EXERCISE 7 Fill in the blanks in this conversation with the correct preposition: *on, in, next to, of, after, out of,* or *for.*

Simon: I'm going to the store ___after___ work. Eggs are on sale—two dozen _____ $3.49.
1.   2.

Marta: Buy bananas too. They're _____ sale—one pound _____ 39 cents.
3.   4.

Simon: That's a good price. Anything else?[1]

Marta: Oh, yes. Buy coffee too.

Simon: Are we _____ coffee? So soon?
5.

Marta: Yes. We drink a lot of coffee.

Simon is _____ the store now. He's _____ the phone with Marta.
6.   7.

Simon: I'm at Tom's Market now. Do we need anything else[1]?

Marta: Yes. Buy some tea. The tea is _____ the coffee. Then come home right away.
8.

Your favorite show is _____ TV at 7!
9.

_____
[1] *Anything else* means anything more.

EXERCISE 8 Fill in the blanks in this phone conversation with the correct preposition: *in, on, at, to,* or *after.*

Sue: Hi, Rick. I'm _____on_____ my cell phone.
1.

Rick: Are you _____ the car?
2.

Sue: No, I'm still _____ work. My shift ends in a few minutes, but I can't come home right now.
3.

_____ work, I have to make a few stops. I can be home _____ about[2] an hour and a half.
4.   5.

Rick: Where do you need to go?

Sue: First, I need to buy gas. Then I have to go _____ the supermarket.
6.

Rick: Can you come home after that?

Sue: No. Then I have to go to the post office. The post office closes _____ 6 p.m.
7.

Rick: Do you have to do all of this now? I'm making dinner. And it's almost ready.

Sue: Oh, that's great, Rick. I can go to the supermarket _____ dinner. And then you can get
8.

gas _____ your way to work.
9.

Rick: Good. Then just stop _____ the post office. And try to get home soon.
10.

---

[2] *About* means it is an estimate. *About an hour and a half* can be ninety minutes, ninety-five minutes, eighty-five minutes, etc.

2

GRAMMAR

There Is and *There Are*—
Affirmative Statements

There Is and *There Are*—
Negative Statements

Quantity Words

CONTEXT

Large Stores and Small Stores

An aisle in a big home supply store

BEFORE YOU READ

1. Are the clerks in stores usually helpful?

2. Do you like to shop in big stores or small stores? Why?

READ

Read the following conversations. Pay special attention to affirmative and negative forms of *there is* and *there are* and quantity words in bold.

CONVERSATION A: At a big home supply store

Sue: You know I don't like to shop at the big hardware store on Saturdays. **There are a lot of** shoppers, and **there's no** place to park.

Rick: Look. **There's** a space over there.

(in the store)

Sue: **There are no** shopping carts.

Rick: We can take a basket. We only need a package of lightbulbs. We need one for the lamp in the living room.

Sue: **There are** so **many** things in this store. It's hard to find anything.

Rick: **There's** a clerk over there. Let's ask him. Excuse me, sir. I need to find lightbulbs.

Clerk: Lightbulbs are in aisle³ 3. **There's** a clerk there. He can help you.

(after visiting aisle 3)

Sue: **There's no** clerk in aisle 3 now. Can you please help us?

Clerk: Sorry. I don't work in aisle 3. That's not my department.

Sue: *(To Rick)* The service here is terrible. **There aren't enough** clerks in this store. No one wants to help us.

Rick: But the prices are good here. And **there are** always coupons for this store in the newspaper. I have a coupon for a package of six lightbulbs for $10. That's 20% off!

CONVERSATION B: In a small hardware store

Clerk: Can I help you?

Peter: Yes. I need lightbulbs.

Clerk: Lightbulbs are downstairs, but **there isn't** an elevator in this store. I can get the lightbulbs for you. Do you want **some** coffee? **There's** a coffee machine over there. It's free for customers.

Peter: Thanks for your help. *(Thinking)* I prefer small stores to big stores. **There's** good service here. **There are** helpful clerks here too. And **there's** free coffee.

> **DID YOU KNOW?**
> Big home supply stores often teach free classes in home repair.

---

³ The pronunciation of *aisle* is /aɪl/. We don't pronounce the *s*.

Vocabulary	Context
home supply store/ hardware store	A **home supply store** and a **hardware store** sell many things for the home: tools, lightbulbs, paint, etc.
shopping cart	We use a **shopping cart** for our items in a store. We push the **cart** down the aisles.
basket	We can use a **basket** for a few items in a store. We carry the basket.
lightbulb	The lamp isn't working. Rick needs to buy a new **lightbulb** for the lamp.
lamp	Sue needs light to read the newspaper. She turns on the **lamp**.
clerk	**Clerk**s work in stores. They help customers.
aisle	**A:** Excuse me. Where are the lightbulbs? **B:** Lightbulbs are in **aisle** 3.
service	Peter likes good **service**. He likes help in a store.
enough	There are a lot of shoppers, but there aren't **enough** clerks.
% (percent) off	The coupon says 40% **(percent) off**. The package of lightbulbs is usually $5. But it's $3 with the coupon.
downstairs	My bedroom is on the second floor, but the kitchen is **downstairs**.
elevator	Peter needs an **elevator** to go downstairs.
prefer	Peter doesn't like big stores. He **prefers** small stores.

LISTEN

 Listen to the sentences about the conversations. Circle *true* or *false*.

CD 2
TR 8

1. (True) False   5. True False

2. True False   6. True False

3. True False   7. True False

4. True False

7.5 *There Is* and *There Are*—Affirmative Statements

Sometimes we use *there is* or *there are* to introduce the subject.

Singular Nouns

There	*Is*	A/An/One	Singular Noun	Prepositional Phrase
There	is	a	parking lot	at the store.
There	is	an	elevator	in the hardware store.
There	is	one	clerk	in aisle 4.

Noncount Nouns

There	*Is*	Quantity Word	Noncount Noun	Prepositional Phrase
There	is		free coffee	for the customers.
There	is	some	milk	near the coffee machine.
There	is	a lot of	sugar	in your coffee.

Language Note:

The contraction for *there is* is **there's**.

Plural Nouns

There	*Are*	Quantity Word	Plural Noun	Prepositional Phrase
There	are		coupons	in the newspaper.
There	are	two	clerks	in aisle 6.
There	are	a lot of	cars	in the parking lot.

Language Note:

There are does not have a contraction.

EXERCISE 1 Fill in the blanks with *there is* or *there are*. Use contractions when possible.

1. _____There are_____ a lot of items in the big store.

2. _____ a sale on lightbulbs this week.

3. _____ a lot of lightbulbs in aisle 3.

4. _____ two elevators in the big store.

5. _____ many shoppers in the big store.

6. _____ a sign near the entrance.

7. _____ coffee for the customers in the small store.

8. _____ good service in the small store.

EXERCISE 2 This is a phone conversation between Simon and Victor. Fill in the blanks with *there is* or *there are*. Use contractions when possible.

Simon: Hello?

Victor: Hi, Simon. It's Victor.

Simon: Are you at home?

Victor: No, I'm not. I'm at the department store[4] with my wife. _____There's_____ a big sale
1.

at this store—50 percent off all winter items. We love sales. We like to save money. Lisa wants to

buy a winter coat. _____ a lot of people in the coat department,
2.

but _____ only one clerk. Where are you?
3.

Simon: I'm at home. _____ a football game on TV.
4.

Victor: I know. And now _____ a long line at the register. I have to wait.
5.

Simon: That's too bad. It's a great game.

Victor: I know. _____ a TV in the store, and _____ some nice
6.   7.

chairs in front of the TV. So I can watch the game too.

Simon: _____ two games today. Let's watch the next game together.
8.

Victor: OK. Sounds great!

7.6 *There Is* and *There Are*—Negative Statements

We can use *there is* and *there are* in negative statements.

Singular Count Nouns

There	Is	No	Singular Count Noun	Prepositional Phrase
There	is	no	coffee machine	in the big store.
There	is	no	elevator	in the big store.
There	is	no	clerk	in aisle 3.

---

[4] A *department store* sells many different things: clothes for men and women, toys, furniture, and more.

Noncount Nouns

There	Isn't	Any	Noncount Noun	Prepositional Phrase
There	isn't	any	space	in the parking lot.
There	isn't	any	coffee	in the big store.
There	isn't	any	time	for shopping now.
There	Is	No	Noncount Noun	Prepositional Phrase
There	is	no	space	in the parking lot.
There	is	no	coffee	in the big store.
There	is	no	time	for shopping now.

Plural Nouns

There	Aren't	Any	Plural Noun	Prepositional Phrase
There	aren't	any	lightbulbs	in this aisle.
There	aren't	any	shopping carts	in the small store.
There	Are	No	Plural Noun	Prepositional Phrase
There	are	no	lightbulbs	in this aisle.
There	are	no	shopping carts	in the small store.

EXERCISE 3 Read the affirmative statement. Complete the negative statement.

1. There's a small hardware store near my house. _____ *There are no* _____ big stores near my house.

2. There are coupons for the big store. _____ coupons for the small store.

3. There are lightbulbs in a hardware store. _____ lightbulbs in a shoe store.

4. There's usually a clerk in aisle 3. _____ clerk in aisle 3 now.

5. There's an elevator in the department store. _____ elevator in the convenience store.

6. There's free coffee in the small store. _____ free coffee in the big store.

7.7 Quantity Words

Quantity	Examples
xxxxxx	There are **many/a lot of** cars in the parking lot.
xxx	There are **some** lamps in aisle 3.
xx (You need xxxx.)	There aren't **enough** clerks in the big store.
x	There is **one/an** elevator in the big store.
0	There aren't **any** lightbulbs in aisle 5.
	There are **no** lightbulbs in aisle 5.

EXERCISE 4 About You Use *there is* or *there are* and the words given to tell about your class and your school. Use quantity words from the chart above. You may have to change the noun to the plural form.

1. copy machine

   A: *There's a copy machine in the library.*

2. book

3. desk for all students

4. Korean students

5. computer

6. young student

7. telephone

8. elevator

9. teacher

EXERCISE 5 About You Fill in the blanks to tell about the place where you live.

1. There aren't enough _____ *windows* _____ in my bedroom.

2. There are no _____ in my neighborhood.

3. There's no _____ in my city.

4. There aren't many _____ in my neighborhood.

5. There are a lot of _____ in my home.

6. There are some _____ in my home.

7. There aren't enough _____ in my bedroom.

8. There's a(n) _____ in my kitchen.

9. There aren't any _____ in my bathroom.

EXERCISE 6 Fill in the blanks with *any, some, many, a lot of, enough, one,* or *no* to complete this conversation. In some cases, more than one answer is possible.

CD 2
TR 10

Sue: Where are the batteries? I need _____ *some* _____ batteries for the flashlight.
1.

Rick: Look in the closet.

Sue: There aren't _____ batteries in the closet.
2.

Rick: Look in the kitchen. There are _____ batteries there, I think.
3.

Sue: There's only _____ battery here. This flashlight needs two batteries. We need to
4.

go to the hardware store and get more batteries.

Rick: Let's go to the home supply store.

Sue: Not again. You know I prefer the small store. In the big store, there aren't _____ clerks to help you. Sometimes I have questions, but there are _____ clerks to answer them. Or I find a clerk and he says, "That's not my department."

Rick: I don't have _____ questions about batteries. A battery is a battery. Look at this section of the newspaper. There are _____ things on sale at the big store— hundreds of things.

Sue: We don't need hundreds of things. We just[5] need batteries.

EXERCISE 7 Fill in the blanks with the missing words from the box below. You can combine two words to fill in some blanks. Use contractions when possible.

CD 2
TR 11

there	they	is	are	it	not	isn't

Rick: Let's go to the hardware store today. _____There's_____ a sale on plants.

_____ really cheap today.

Sue: Let's go to the bookstore. _____ a sale on all travel books.

_____ 50% off. Let's go to the bookstore first and then to the hardware store.

Rick: _____ enough time. It's almost 4:00. The hardware store closes at 5:30.

_____ Saturday, and the hardware store _____ open late on Saturday.

Sue: The small hardware store _____ open late, but the home supply store is open.

You know, I don't really want to go to the hardware store with you. _____

always too crowded. I have an idea. You can go to the hardware store, and I can go to the bookstore.

I need something to read.

Rick: Need or want? You have a lot of books.

Sue: _____ all old. I need new books.

Rick: And I need some plants.

---

[5] *Just* means only.

3

GRAMMAR

There Is and *There Are—Yes/No* Questions

There Is and *There Are—Wh-* Questions

CONTEXT

Smart Shopping

A woman compares the prices of rugs.

BEFORE YOU READ

1. Is it easy to make choices in a store? Why or why not?

2. Do you compare prices when you shop?

READ

Read the following conversation. Pay special attention to *yes/no* questions and *wh-* questions using *there is* and *there are* in bold.

Halina and her husband, Peter, are in the supermarket.

Peter: There are many brands of shampoo. **Why are there** so many brands? Do people need so many choices?

Halina: I don't think so. **Is there** a difference between this shampoo for $2.99 and that shampoo for $7.99?

Peter: I don't know. Let's buy the cheap one.

Halina: OK. There's probably no difference.

Peter: **Are there** any other items on the shopping list?

Halina: Just two. We need sugar. The sugar is in aisle 6.

We need:

bread, sugar

rice, cheese

fruit, milk

shampoo

aspirin

dog food

(in aisle 6)

Halina: This sign says 25 ounces for $1.75. That one says five pounds for $2.25. Which one is a better buy?

Peter: I don't know. What's an ounce?

Halina: It's part of a pound.

Peter: **How many ounces are there** in a pound?

Halina: Sixteen.

Peter: **Is there** a calculator on your phone?

Halina: Yes, but we don't need it. Look. There's a small sign under the sugar. The five-pound bag is about 2.8¢ an ounce. The 25-ounce bag is about 7¢ an ounce. The big bag is a better buy.

Peter: You're a smart shopper. Are we finished? **Is there** anything else on the list?

Halina: Yes. There's one more thing—dog food.

Peter: Wow! Look. There are over 20 kinds of dog food.

Halina: Dogs have choices too.

DID YOU KNOW?
One pound = .45 kilograms
One ounce = 28.35 grams

Vocabulary	Context
brand	Many companies make soap. There are a lot of different **brands**.
shampoo	I need to buy **shampoo**. I need to wash my hair.
choice	There are 20 kinds of dog food, so there are many **choices**. We have to pick one.
difference between	What's the **difference between** the cheap shampoo and the expensive one? The expensive shampoo is better quality.
ounce	An **ounce** is a unit of measure. Sixteen **ounces** is equal to one pound.
calculator	I have a **calculator** on my phone. It helps me do math.
better buy	The large bag of sugar is a **better buy**. We can save money.

LISTEN

CD 2 TR 13

Listen to the sentences about the conversation. Circle *true* or *false*.

1. (True)   False
2. True   False
3. True   False
4. True   False
5. True   False
6. True   False
7. True   False

7.8 *There Is* and *There Are—Yes/No* Questions

Compare statements and questions with *there is* and *there are*.

Statement	Question	Short Answer
There's a shampoo aisle.	**Is there** a hardware aisle in this store?	No, there isn't.
There are large bags of sugar.	**Are there** any small bags of sugar?	Yes, there are.
There's dog food in this aisle.	**Is there** any cat food in this aisle?	Yes, there is.

Language Notes:

1. We often use *any* in questions with noncount and plural count nouns.

2. We don't make a contraction in an affirmative short answer.

    Yes, there is.   NOT: Yes, there's.

EXERCISE 1 Complete the short answers.

1. Are there any clerks in the store? Yes, _____*there are*_____ .

2. Is there a price on the shampoo bottles? No, _____ .

3. Are there a lot of shoppers in the store? Yes, _____ .

4. Is there any dog food on sale this week? No, _____ .

5. Are there a lot of choices of dog food? Yes, _____ .

6. Is there a coupon for sugar? Yes, _____ .

7. Are there any shopping carts in this store? No, _____ .

EXERCISE 2 Complete the questions.

1. _____*Is there*_____ good service in a small store?

2. _____ any shoppers in the checkout line?

3. _____ a clerk in the cereal aisle?

4. _____ any space in the parking lot?

5. _____ any coupons for shampoo in the newspaper?

6. _____ an elevator in the supermarket?

7. _____ a lot of shoppers today?

EXERCISE 3 Work with a partner. Ask a question with *is there* or *are there any* and the words given. Your partner will answer.

1. an elevator/in this building

   A: Is there an elevator in this building?

   B: No, there isn't.

2. Mexican students/in this class

3. new words/in this lesson

4. photos/on this page

5. a verb chart/in your dictionary

6. hard exercises/in this lesson

7. a computer lab/at this school

8. restrooms/on this floor

9. a gym/at this school

10. a library/in your town

7.9 *There Is* and *There Are*—*Wh-* Questions

PART A: *How much, how many,* and *why* are common question words with *is there* and *are there.* Notice question word order.

Question Word(s)	Be	There	Phrase	Answer
How much sugar	**is**	**there**	in the bag?	One pound.
How many ounces	**are**	**there**	in a pound?	Sixteen.
Why	**are**	**there**	20 different kinds of shampoo?	I don't know.

PART B: Compare *yes/no* questions and *wh-* questions.

Yes/No Questions	Wh- Questions
Are there ten items on the list?	How many items **are there** on the list?
Are there different kinds of shampoo?	Why **are there** different kinds of shampoo?
Are there many kinds of dog food?	How many kinds of dog food **are there**?
Is there a difference between this shampoo and that shampoo?	Why **is there** a difference in price?

EXERCISE 4 Read the statements. Write *wh-* questions with the words given.

1. There are ten kinds of shampoo.

   How many <u>kinds of shampoo are there?</u>

2. There are a lot of people in this line.

   Why _____

3. There are 16 ounces in a pound.

   How many _____

4. There are a few items on the list.

   How many _____

5. There are many brands of dog food.

   Why _____

6. There's some sugar in this bag.

   How much _____

7. There is a pharmacy in the store.

   Why _____

8. There's a lot of time left.

   How much _____

EXERCISE 5 **About You** Work with a partner. Use the following words to ask and answer questions about your class or school. Use *how much* or *how many* in your questions.

1. desks/in this room

   A: How many desks are there in this room?

   B: There are 20 desks in this room.

2. students/in this class

3. windows/in this room

4. paper/on the floor

5. telephones/in this room

6. men's restrooms/on this floor

7. floors/in this building

8. pages/in this book

9. new vocabulary/on this page

10. photos/this unit

EXERCISE 6 Write questions and answers for the items in the box below.

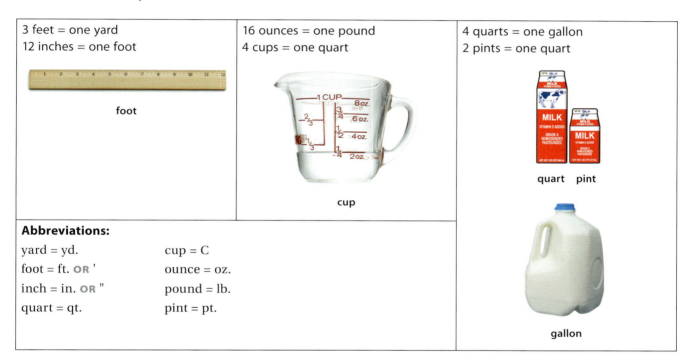

3 feet = one yard	16 ounces = one pound	4 quarts = one gallon
12 inches = one foot	4 cups = one quart	2 pints = one quart
foot	cup	quart pint

Abbreviations:

yard = yd.	cup = C
foot = ft. **OR** '	ounce = oz.
inch = in. **OR** "	pound = lb.
quart = qt.	pint = pt.

gallon

1. How many feet are there in a yard?

   There are 3 feet in a yard.

2. _____

   _____

3. _____

   _____

4. _____

   _____

continued

Lesson 3   Smart Shopping   **169**

5. _____

   _____

6. _____

   _____

EXERCISE 7 Fill in the blanks with the missing words from the box below. You can use some items more
than once. Use contractions when possible.

CD 2
TR 14

there is	there are	is there	are there	how many

Ali: I'm going for a walk.

Shafia: Wait. I need a few things at the supermarket. Let me look at my shopping list.

Ali: How many items _____*are there*_____?
                                              1.

Shafia: About ten. Also go to the office supply store. I need some pens.

Ali: Where's the office supply store?

Shafia: _____ a few office supply stores near here. _____ one
                        2.   **3.**
              next to the supermarket on Elm Street.

Ali: _____ pens _____ in a box?
                        4.   **5.**

Shafia: You can buy a box of 20.

Ali: _____ anything else on your list?
                        6.

Shafia: Yes, _____. We need paper for the printer too. Please buy two reams[6] of paper.
                        7.

Ali: _____ sheets of paper _____ in one ream?
                        8.   **9.**

Shafia: Five hundred, I think.

Ali: What about printer ink? _____ enough ink in the cartridge?[7]
                                              10.

Shafia: I don't think so. Please get some ink too.

---

[6] A *ream* is a package of paper with 500 sheets.

[7] Ink for the printer comes in a *cartridge*.

🎧 **EXERCISE 8** Fill in the blanks to complete the conversation. Use *there is, there are, is there,* or *are there.*
CD 2 / TR 15   Use contractions when possible.

Marta: The kids need new coats. Let's go shopping today. _____There's_____ a 12-hour sale at
1.

Baker's Department Store—today only.

Simon: _____ a sale on men's coats too?
2.

Marta: Yes, _____ . _____ a lot of great things on sale:
3.   4.

winter[8] coats, sweaters, boots, gloves, and more.

Simon: How do you always know about all the sales in town?

Marta: _____ an ad in the store window. It says, "End of winter sale.
5.

All winter items 50% off."

Simon: Why _____ a sale on winter things? It's still winter.
6.

Marta: Spring is almost here[9].

Simon: It's only January. It's so cold. _____ two or three more months of winter.
7.

Marta: You're right! But stores need space for new things for the spring.

_____

[8] The four seasons are: *winter, spring, summer,* and *fall.*

[9] *Almost here* means very close in time.

WRITING

PART 1 Editing Advice

1. Use the correct preposition.

   Sue likes to shop ~~in the~~ *at* night.

   Your favorite program begins ~~after~~ *in* 20 minutes.

2. Don't use prepositions with certain time expressions.

   Simon works five days ~~in~~ a week.

3. Don't use *to* after *near*.

   There's a convenience store near ~~to~~ my house.

4. Don't write a contraction for *there are*.

   ~~There're~~ *There are* 20 students in the class.

5. Don't use *a* after *there are*.

   There are ~~a~~ good sales this week.

6. Don't use a double negative.

   There aren't ~~no~~ *any* lightbulbs in this aisle.

7. Use correct word order.

   How many batteries ~~there are~~ *are there* in the flashlight?

PART 2 Editing Practice

Some of the shaded words and phrases have mistakes. Find the mistakes and correct them. If the shaded words are correct, write *C*.

Ali: I need a lightbulb for this lamp. Are there *C* any extra lightbulbs?
1.

Shafia: No, there isn't *aren't*. We need to buy more.
2.

Ali: Let's go in the hardware store. Is it open now?
3.

Shafia: No. It's late. The hardware store isn't open in the night. It closes in 6:00 p.m. But the big store
4.   5.

near to the bank is open very late.
6.

Ali: There are a lot of things in sale at that store. Let's make a list.
7.   8.   9.

Shafia: We don't need a lot of things. We only need lightbulbs.

Ali: What about batteries?[10] Are there a batteries in the house?
10.   11.

Shafia: There're some AA batteries.
12.

Ali: But we need C batteries for the radio.

Shafia: There aren't no C batteries in the house.
13.

Ali: Do you want to go to the store with me?
14.

Shafia: My favorite show starts after five minutes. Can you go alone?
15.

Ali: OK.

Shafia: There's no rice in the house. Can you get some rice too?
16.

Ali: There isn't any rice at the hardware store.
17.

Shafia: Of course not. But the hardware store is next the supermarket. In fact, you don't need
18.

the hardware store at all. There are a lightbulbs and batteries at the supermarket too.
19.   20.

Ali: There's no need to go to two stores. Is this supermarket open at night?
21.   22.

Shafia: Yes. It's open seven days in a week. And it's open all night.
23.   24.

PART 3 Write About It

Write five or six sentences to describe each photo. You can write affirmative statements, negative statements, or questions.

> In photo A, there is one customer in the aisle.
>
> Why is she at the hardware store?

PART 4 Learner's Log

1. Write one sentence about each of these topics:
   - Shopping in the United States
   - Different types of stores
   - Getting a good price

2. Write any questions you still have about shopping in the United States.

---

[10] Batteries come in different sizes. For example, AA and C.

A tourist mails a postcard in the
Galapagos Islands, Ecuador.

ERRANDS

What you do today can improve
all your tomorrows.

— Ralph Marston

1

GRAMMAR

The Present Continuous— Affirmative Statements

Spelling Rules of the -ing Form

The Present Continuous— Use

The Present Continuous— Negative Statements

CONTEXT

At the Post Office

A woman prepares a package at a U.S. post office.

BEFORE YOU READ

1. What services does the U.S. post office have? What does it sell?

2. Do you send packages to your country? Why or why not?

READ

CD 2 TR 16

Lisa is at the post office today. She's writing an email to a friend on her phone as she waits. Read her email. Pay special attention to the present continuous in bold.

Hi Rosa,

It's Friday morning and I**'m practicing** my English. People **are doing** errands. I'm at the post office. Many things **are happening** at the post office. The clerks are very busy. Many people **are waiting** in line. They**'re not getting** fast service today. But they **aren't complaining**.

A customer at the counter has two packages. There is a clerk behind the counter. The clerk **is weighing** one package. He**'s using** a scale. The customer **is holding** the second package. He **isn't paying** for the postage in cash. He**'s using** his credit card.

My friend Marta **is picking up** a package. Amy is with her. Amy **is holding** Marta's hand. Marta **is giving** her identification (ID) to the clerk.

A customer **is using** the automated postal center. He **isn't waiting** in line. He**'s mailing** a package, and he**'s weighing** the package on the scale. He**'s paying** by credit card. The machine **is printing** the postage label. Self-service is fast.

A customer **is buying** stamps from a stamp machine. He**'s paying** in cash. He**'s not using** coins. He**'s putting** a ten-dollar bill in the stamp machine. Stamp machines in the post office give coins for change. This man **is getting** some one-dollar coins in change. Nobody **is buying** mailing supplies today.

Are you free today? Can you get lunch?

Lisa

DID YOU KNOW?
People in the United States send about 160 billion pieces of mail each year. The United States Postal Service handles about 40% of the world's mail.

Vocabulary	Context
do errands	Marta has to **do errands** today. She's going to the post office and the bank.
wait in line	The **line** is long. The customers have to **wait in line**.
complain	The customers aren't happy. They are **complaining**.
customer	There are many **customers** in the post office. One **customer** is buying stamps.
counter	The clerks work behind the **counter** at the post office.
package	One customer is sending a **package**. It is a present for his mother's birthday.
weigh	The clerk is **weighing** a customer's package. The package **weighs** two pounds.
scale	We use a **scale** to weigh things.
hold	A customer is **holding** a package. He has the package in his hands. Marta is **holding** Amy's hand.
postage	When we mail a package, we have to pay **postage**.
pick up	Marta is **picking up** her mail.
automated postal center	We can weigh our packages and pay for postage at the **automated postal center**. We don't need a clerk.
print	In the automated postal center, a machine weighs a package. It also **prints** the postage.
self-service	You don't need a clerk to buy stamps. You can use a machine. It's **self-service**.
stamp	When we mail a letter, we put a **stamp** on it. A **stamp** shows the postage.
mailing supplies	**Mailing supplies** are boxes and envelopes.

LISTEN

CD 2
TR 17

Listen to the sentences about the activities in the post office. Circle *true* or *false*.

1. (True)   False   6. True   False

2. True   False   7. True   False

3. True   False   8. True   False

4. True   False   9. True   False

5. True   False

8.1 The Present Continuous—Affirmative Statements

We form the present continuous with a form of *be* + verb *-ing*.

Subject	Be	Verb *-ing*	
I	**am**	**mailing**	a letter.
Dorota	**is**	**waiting**	in line.
Nobody	**is**	**buying**	mailing supplies.
We	**are**	**using**	the stamp machine.
You	**are**	**picking up**	a package.
The clerks	**are**	**standing**	behind the counter.

Language Notes:

1. We can make contractions with a pronoun + *be*.

   I'm mailing a letter.

   She's waiting in line.

   We're using the stamp machine.

2. We can make contractions with a singular noun + *is*.

   Lisa's writing an email.

3. There is no contraction for a plural noun + *are*.

EXERCISE 1 Fill in the blanks with the present continuous. Use contractions when possible. Use the ideas from the reading and the verbs from the box. Answers may vary.

pick	give	weigh	help	pay	stand	buy ✓	wait	do

1. One customer *'s buying* _____ some stamps.

2. Amy _____ next to Marta.

3. Many people _____ in line.

4. Marta _____ her ID to the postal clerk.

5. Marta _____ a package.

6. The clerks _____ the customers.

7. A customer _____ a package at the automated postal center.

8. A lot of people _____ errands today.

9. Some customers _____ in cash.

8.2 Spelling Rules of the *-ing* Form

Verb	*-ing* Form	Rule
go eat look	go**ing** eat**ing** look**ing**	In most cases, we add *-ing* to the base form.
sit plan	sit**ting** plan**ning**	If a one-syllable verb ends in consonant + vowel + consonant, we double the last consonant. Then we add *-ing*.
give write	giv**ing** writ**ing**	If the verb ends in a consonant + *e*, we drop the *e*. Then we add *-ing*. NOT: giveing Do not double the last consonant after you drop the *e*. NOT: writting
show fix pay	show**ing** fix**ing** pay**ing**	We don't double final *w, x,* or *y.* We just add *-ing*. NOT: showwing, fixxing, payying

EXERCISE 2 Fill in the blanks with the present continuous of the verb given. Spell the *-ing* form correctly. Use contractions when possible.

1. Marta ___'s picking___ up a package.
   _{pick}

2. A few customers _____ some stamps from a machine.
   _{get}

3. Amy _____ with Marta.
   _{wait}

4. The clerk _____ a customer's credit card.
   _{take}

5. Marta and Amy _____ in line.
   _{stand}

6. They _____ at the people in the post office.
   _{look}

7. Two customers _____ machines.
   _{use}

8. A man _____ money in the stamp machine.
   _{put}

9. One customer _____ a package.
   _{weigh}

10. Nobody _____ to buy mailing supplies.
    _{plan}

11. Marta _____ her ID to a clerk.
    _{give}

12. Lisa _____ an email now.
    _{write}

8.3 The Present Continuous—Use

Examples	Explanation
People **are buying** stamps now.	The action is happening now, at this time.
Halina**'s standing** near the counter. Marta and Amy **are holding** hands. Nobody**'s buying** envelopes.	The verbs *stand*, *sleep*, *sit*, *wear*, *hold*, and *wait* have no action. We use the present continuous to describe a present situation.
I**'m working** overtime this week. Lisa**'s learning** some new words today.	The action is happening during a specific present time period.

Language Note:

Some common time expressions with the present continuous are: *now, right now, at the moment, at this time, today, all day, this week,* and *this month*.

EXERCISE 3 Write two sentences about each picture with verbs from the box. Answers may vary.

stand	wait	wear	play	hold	give	take	write	use
leave	work	pick up	go	buy	put	mail	get	sit

1. This man is going into the post office.

   He's holding some envelopes.

2. _____

   _____

3. _____

   _____

4. _____

   _____

5. _____

   _____

continued

6. _____

_____

7. _____

_____

8.4 The Present Continuous—Negative Statements

Subject	Be + Not	Verb -ing	
I	**am not**	**getting**	mailing supplies.
You	**are not**	**buying**	stamps.
Marta	**is not**	**going**	to the bank.
Halina and Dorota	**are not**	**talking**	to the clerk.

Language Note:

We can make negative contractions with *be*.

     I'm not waiting in line. (There's only one contraction for *I am not*.)

     Marta**'s not** using the stamp machine.   She **isn't** mailing a letter.

     We**'re not** buying supplies.   We **aren't** mailing a package.

EXERCISE 4 Read the first sentence. Then write a negative sentence with the words given. Use contractions when possible.

1. Marta is picking up a package.

   She's not talking to Amy now. OR She isn't talking to Amy now._____
                                 talk to Amy now

2. A customer is buying stamps.

   _____
                               use his credit card

3. Many people are waiting in line.

   _____
                       complain about the service

4. Halina and Dorota are waiting for service.

   _____
                        use self-service

5. Lisa is writing in her journal.

   _____
                       mail a package

6. Halina is doing errands alone today.

_____

shop with Peter

EXERCISE 5 About You Use the words given to write true sentences about your activities at the present time. Make an affirmative or negative statement. If you write a negative statement, write a true affirmative statement also. Use contractions when possible.

1. I/do errands now

I'm not doing errands now. I'm doing an exercise in English.

2. We/use pencils now

We're using pencils now.

3. I/write an email

_____

4. The teacher/wear sneakers

_____

5. We/use a dictionary

_____

6. The teacher/look at my ID

_____

7. We/talk about the supermarket

_____

8. The students/complain about this exercise

_____

9. I/try to learn all the new words

_____

10. The teacher/help me now

_____

EXERCISE 6 Marta has her package now. She's leaving the post office. She sees Dorota and Halina. Read their conversation. Then write sentences about the conversation. Use the present continuous, affirmative and/or negative. Answers will vary.

Marta: Hi, Dorota. It's nice to see you, Halina. How are you?

Halina: I'm fine, thanks. It's good to see you, Marta.

Dorota: Hi, Marta. I'm mailing this package to my son. He's in college now. He's living in Canada this year. As usual, this line isn't moving very fast.

Marta: Did you know the post office has services online now? The website has prices for all packages. You can print the postage and you can pay for it online with your credit card. Then you can give the package to your mail carrier the next day. It costs the same. And it's fast!

Dorota: I know. But I can't weigh the package at home. I don't have a scale. I need to send this package today. My son's waiting for his winter clothes.

Marta: The post office has a new automated postal center. You can weigh the package and pay for postage from a machine now. It's over there. And nobody's waiting.

Dorota: That's OK. It's my turn now.

Marta: Amy and I are going to lunch now. Do you both want to come with us?

Halina: I'm sorry. We can't. Peter's waiting for us outside in the car.

_____

_____

_____

_____

EXERCISE 7 Complete the short conversations with the affirmative or negative of the verb given in the present continuous. Use contractions when possible.

1. **A:** Can I use your computer?

   B: Sorry, I 'm using _____ it at the moment. Can you wait?

      use

2. **A:** Can you mail this letter for me?

   B: Sorry, I _____ home today. I _____ to the post office.

      a. stay   **b.** go

3. **A:** Why can't Dorota do these errands with you now?

   B: Her friend _____ her today.

      visit

4. **A:** I need help at the post office.

   B: Victor _____ today. He can go with you.

      work

5. **A:** Why can't I use the phone right now?

   B: Because I _____ to make an important call.

      plan

6. **A:** What's wrong[1] with this stamp machine?

   B: I don't know. But it _____ right today. Let's wait in line for a clerk.

      work

7. **A:** This post office is very busy right now.

   B: Yes. A lot of people _____ in line.

      wait

8. **A:** Look at the line at the counter. It's too long.

   B: But nobody _____ the automated postal center. Let's use that.

      use

9. **A:** I _____ the directions correctly. But it _____ the

      a. follow   **b.** print
   postage label. What's wrong?

   B: I don't know. Let's ask the clerk.

---

[1] *What's wrong?* asks about a problem.

2

GRAMMAR

The Present Continuous—
  Yes/No Questions
The Present Continuous—
  Wh- Questions
The Present Continuous—
  Subject Questions

CONTEXT

Drive-Throughs

A woman uses the drive-through at a bank.

BEFORE YOU READ

1. Are there any drive-throughs in your neighborhood?

2. Which drive-throughs do you use?

READ

CD 2
TR 18

Read the following conversation. Pay special attention to *yes/no* questions and *wh-* questions using the present continuous in bold.

Amy:	**Are we going** home now, Mommy?
Marta:	Not yet. I still have a few errands.
Amy:	**Where are we going** now?
Marta:	To the bank. I need some quarters for the washing machine. I can get a roll of quarters at the bank.
Amy:	**Why are you turning** here? The bank's over there.
Marta:	I'm using the drive-through, and it's right here.
Amy:	There's someone ahead of us. **What's she doing**? **Is she getting** quarters too?
Marta:	I don't know. She's probably getting money. Or maybe she's cashing a check.
Amy:	**Who's talking**? I hear someone.
Marta:	That's the teller. She's behind the window. She's using a microphone.
Amy:	**What's that man doing** over there?
Marta:	He's sending a deposit to the teller at the window. There's money or checks in that envelope. He is depositing money into his account.
Amy:	**What's he holding**?
Marta:	It's a tube. It's a place for his deposit. He can put checks or cash in the tube, and a machine takes the tube to the teller.
Amy:	**Is the teller helping** both customers at the same time?
Marta:	Yes.

DID YOU KNOW?

Many businesses have drive-throughs: banks, restaurants, and pharmacies. Sometimes signs use the informal spelling, *drive-thru*.

Vocabulary	Context
drive-through	Marta and Amy are using a **drive-through**. They don't have to get out of the car for service.
roll	You can get a **roll** of quarters at a bank.
turn	They are **turning** into the drive-through.
ahead of	Three people are **ahead of** us in line. We have to wait.
probably	That customer is giving money to the teller. He's **probably** making a deposit.
maybe	She is at the bank. **Maybe** she needs to take out money. I'm not sure.
cash a check	The woman has a check. She needs **cash**. She's **cashing** her **check** at the bank.
teller	A **teller** is helping a customer at the bank.
microphone	The teller is using a **microphone** to talk to people.
deposit (v.) deposit (n.)	We put money in the bank. We **deposit** money. The man is making a **deposit** in the bank.
tube	A customer is using a **tube** to send a deposit to the teller.

LISTEN

CD 2
TR 19

Listen to the questions about the conversation. Circle *true* or *false*.

1. (True) False   5. True   False

2. True   False   6. True   False

3. True   False   7. True   False

4. True   False   8. True   False

8.5 The Present Continuous—*Yes/No* Questions

Be	Subject	Verb *-ing*		Short Answer
Am	I	**using**	the right envelope?	Yes, you are.
Are	you	**talking**	to the teller?	Yes, I am.
Is	Halina	**going**	into the bank?	No, she isn't.
Are	we	**turning**	here?	No, we're not.
Are	they	**waiting**	in their cars?	Yes, they are.

EXERCISE 1 Write a *yes/no* question with the words given. Answer the question with a short answer. Use the ideas from the conversation on page 187.

1. Amy/talk to her mother

    Is Amy talking to her mother? Yes, she is.

2. Marta and Amy/use the drive-through

_____

3. Marta/cash a check

_____

4. Marta and Amy/wait in the car

_____

5. Marta/answer Amy's questions

_____

6. the teller/help Marta now

_____

7. the man/hold the tube

_____

8. the man/ask for a roll of quarters

_____

9. two customers/get service at the same time

_____

EXERCISE 2 About You Use the words given to ask a partner questions about what he or she is doing. Your partner will answer with a short answer first and then add information. Write the questions and answers for practice.

1. you/speak English

A: Are you speaking English now? _____

B: Yes, I am. I'm using the present continuous. _____

2. you/ask for help

A: _____

B: _____

3. someone/help you

A: _____

B: _____

continued

4. your teacher/grade your work

   A: _____

   B: _____

5. you/write in your book

   A: _____

   B: _____

6. your teacher/stand in front of the class

   A: _____

   B: _____

7. you/learn a lot of new words today

   A: _____

   B: _____

8. you/wait for something

   A: _____

   B: _____

9. you/sit at a desk

   A: _____

   B: _____

10. your classmates/complain about something

   A: _____

   B: _____

8.6 The Present Continuous—*Wh*- Questions

Question Word(s)	Be	Subject	Verb -*ing*		Short Answer
What	**are**	you	**doing**?		Waiting for service.
Where	**is**	he	**going**?		To the drive-through.
How many people	**is**	the teller	**helping**?		Two.
Who	**is**	the teller	**helping**?		A man and a woman.
How	**are**	some customers	**making**	a deposit?	In a tube.
Why	**are**	people	**using**	the drive-through?	Because it's easy and fast.

Language Notes:

1. Sometimes a preposition (*about, to*, etc.) comes at the end of a question.

2. Remember, we can make a contraction with some question words and *is*.

    What's Amy asking about?

EXERCISE 3 Complete each of the short conversations. Write a question for the each answer given. Use the question words: *who, what, where, why, how many*, and *how*. The underlined phrase is the answer.

1. **A.** <u>What is Amy asking Marta?</u>

   B. Amy's asking Marta <u>about the drive-through</u>.

2. **A.** _____

   B. Two customers are waiting in line <u>at the drive-through pharmacy</u>.

3. **A.** _____

   B. Marta is waiting for <u>some quarters</u> at the bank.

4. **A.** _____

   B. She is expecting to get <u>one</u> roll of quarters.

5. **A.** _____

   B. The customer is putting a deposit <u>in a tube</u>.

6. **A.** _____

   B. Halina and Peter are learning <u>how to use the machine</u>.

7. **A.** _____

   B. <u>Because we have a test tomorrow</u>.

continued

8. **A.** _____

   B. The teller is helping <u>one</u> customer at the moment.

9. **A.** _____

   B. Simon and Victor are talking about <u>the bank</u>.

10. **A.** _____

    B. <u>Because it's easy and convenient to use the drive-through</u>.

EXERCISE 4 Complete the conversation between Marta and Amy at the fast-food restaurant drive-through. Use the words and expressions from the box.

CD 2
TR 20

| are waiting | he's asking | is putting | what are you ordering | why are we going | how is it doing ✓ |

Amy: Mommy, the sign is talking. _____<u>How is it doing</u>_____ that?
1.

Marta: It's not the sign. It's the clerk. Look. He's over there behind the window. _____
2.

and for our order.²

Amy: _____ ?
3.

Marta: A chicken sandwich and a salad. And some milk too. What about you?

Amy: Ummmmmm.

Marta: Hurry, Amy. The clerk's waiting. And customers _____ behind us.
4.

Amy: Ummmm. I want a grilled cheese!

Marta: (*speaking to the clerk*) One chicken sandwich, one grilled cheese, one salad, and

two cartons of milk, please.

Server: That's $12.79. Please go to the next window.

Amy: _____ there?
5.

Marta: To pay and to pick up our food. Look. The clerk

_____ our lunch in a bag.
6.

Server: Seven dollars and 21 cents is your change.

Thank you. Have a good day.

_____
² An *order* is a list of food people want from a restaurant.

192 Unit 8

8.7 The Present Continuous—Subject Questions

Question Word(s)	Be	Verb		Answer
Who	is	talking?		Amy and Marta are.
What	is	happening	at the bank?	Customers are doing business.
Which customer	is	waiting	in line?	Marta is.
How many customers	are	getting	quarters now?	One customer is.

Language Notes:

1. We use a plural verb (*are*) after *how many*, even if the answer is singular.

2. We use a singular verb (*is*) after *who*, even if the answer is plural.

3. We use a noun after *which* and *how many/much*.

EXERCISE 5 Write a question for each answer given. Use the question words *who, which, what,* and *how many* as subjects. The underlined word or phrase is the answer.

1. Which customer is using the tube? OR Who is using the tube?

    A man is using the tube.

2. _____

    The teller is using a microphone.

3. _____

    One customer is making a deposit.

4. _____

    A man and a woman are getting help now.

5. _____

    Something is happening at the bank.

6. _____

    Three customers are using the drive-through.

7. _____

    A tube is taking the man's deposit to the teller.

8. _____

    An accident is stopping traffic up ahead.

WRITING

PART 1 Editing Advice

1. Always use a form of *be* with the present continuous.

   He ^is working at that store.

2. Don't forget to use the *-ing* form with present continuous verbs.

   Marta and Amy ~~are wait~~ *are waiting* at the drive-through.

3. Use the correct word order in a question.

   What ~~he is~~ *is he* doing there?

4. Don't use the present continuous for usual or customary actions.

   Sometimes Simon ~~is working~~ *works* on Saturdays.

5. Follow the spelling rules for the *-ing* form.

   A clerk is ~~takeing~~ *taking* a customer's order.

   Maya is ~~showwing~~ *showing* Lisa her art project.

PART 2 Editing Practice

Some of the shaded words and phrases have mistakes. Find the mistakes and correct them. If the shaded words are correct, write *C*.

Amy and Marta continue their conversation in the car.

Amy: Why ~~you are~~ *are you* turning here?
  1.

Marta: I need to stop at the pharmacy. A lot of cars are waiting *C* at the drive-through. Let's go inside.
  2.

Amy: But usually you're using the drive-through. Why are we go inside now?
  3. **4.**

Marta: The drive-through is very busy and I want to talk to a pharmacy clerk.

(inside, at the pharmacy counter)

Amy: That woman's wearing a white coat. Is she a doctor?
  5.

Marta: No. She's a pharmacist. She's busy. She talking to a customer. We have to wait.
  6.

Amy: What are they talking about?
  7.

Marta: That customer's buying aspirin. Maybe he asking about different brands of aspirin.
8.   9.

Or maybe the pharmacist's giveing the customer advice. Now it's our turn.
10.

(in the car again)

Marta: What are you doing, Amy?
11.

Amy: I'm hungry. I'm eat my grilled cheese now.
12.

PART 3 Write About It

Look at the picture. Write a paragraph of five or six sentences about what is or isn't happening.

Simon is working on his computer. He isn't going to the post office today.

PART 4 Learner's Log

1. Write one sentence about each of these topics:
   - U.S. post office services
   - Drive-through businesses

2. Write any questions you still have about the post office or drive-through businesses in the United States.

CHANGES

Weather changes quickly as clouds and
lightning move into a clear sky.

To improve is to change; to be
perfect is to change often.

— Winston Churchill

1

GRAMMAR

The Future—
   Affirmative Statements

The Future—
   Negative Statements

The Future—Use

Time Expressions

CONTEXT

Getting Ready for a
New Baby

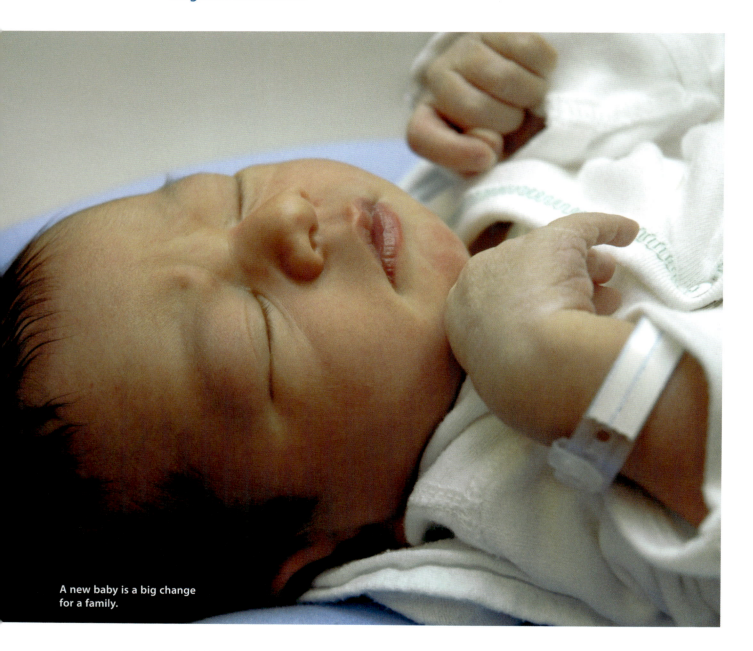

A new baby is a big change
for a family.

BEFORE YOU READ

1. What do parents have to buy for a new baby?

2. What changes in family life are necessary for a new baby?

READ

CD 2
TR 21

Read the following conversation. Pay special attention to affirmative and negative statements with *be going to* and time expressions in bold.

Shafia and her husband, Ali, **are going to have** a baby in November. Dorota and Halina are visiting Shafia. Ali is at work.

Shafia: Our baby**'s going to arrive in two months**. I'm not ready.

Dorota: Let's see. You**'re going to need** a crib, a high chair, and a car seat.

Halina: You can use my daughter's crib. She's two now, and she has a bed. She also has a new car seat. We**'re not going to need** the crib or the car seat anymore.

Shafia: That's wonderful, Halina. Thank you. I**'m not going to need** the car seat **for a while**. We don't have a car right now.

Dorota: Actually, you need one to take the baby home from the hospital. And you**'re going to need** a stroller to take the baby outside. There's a resale shop for kids in my neighborhood. You can get a high chair and a stroller there. Resale shops are not expensive.

Shafia: What's a resale shop, Dorota?

Dorota: It's a store with used items. People take their used clothing and furniture there. The shop sells them at a low price. The money often goes to a charity. Resale shops are very popular.

Shafia: That's a great idea. We can go on Thursday.

Dorota: Good idea. But don't buy too many clothes for the baby. People **are going to give** you gifts.

Shafia: You're right. We have a lot of relatives. We**'re not going to buy** too much.

Halina: You**'re going to need** some help **for the first weeks** too. New babies are a lot of work. And you**'re not going to get** much sleep.

Shafia: I know. My mother**'s going to help**. She**'s going to stay** with us **for the first month**. She's so excited. She**'s going to be** a grandmother for the first time.

> ### DID YOU KNOW?
> The average age of first-time mothers is going up. Today it is about 26 years old.

Vocabulary	Context
arrive	Ali isn't home now. He's going to **arrive** at 6 p.m.
crib	Babies sleep in **cribs**.
high chair	Babies sit in a **high chair** to eat.
wonderful	I'm so happy about your new job. That's **wonderful** news.
for a while	She's going to stay here **for a while**. I don't know how long.
stroller	You can take a baby outside in a **stroller**.
resale shop	You can buy good used items at a **resale shop**, sometimes called a thrift store.
used	This furniture is not new. It's **used**.
furniture	She needs baby **furniture**: a crib and a high chair.

continued

charity	The resale shop gives money to a **charity**. The **charity** helps sick children.
gift	Relatives and friends are going to buy **gifts** for the baby.
relative	She is my husband's sister. She is a **relative** of our family.
get some sleep	I'm tired. I need to **get some sleep**. I **don't get much sleep** these days. I have a new baby.
excited	My family is **excited** about the baby. They're very happy.

LISTEN

CD 2
TR 22

Listen to the sentences about the conversation. Circle *true* or *false*.

1. True	(False)		**6.** True	False		
2. True	False		**7.** True	False		
3. True	False		**8.** True	False		
4. True	False		**9.** True	False		
5. True	False					

9.1 The Future—Affirmative Statements

Be Going To Forms

Subject	Be	Going To	Verb (Base Form)	
I	**am**	**going to**	**need**	some help.
My mother	**is**	**going to**	**help**	me.
We	**are**	**going to**	**have**	a baby.
You	**are**	**going to**	**give**	us a crib.
Shafia and Ali	**are**	**going to**	**buy**	a used high chair.
Their relatives	**are**	**going to**	**help**	them.
There	**is**	**going to**	**be**	a change in Shafia's life.

Pronunciation Note:

In informal speech, we pronounce *going to* as /gənə/. Listen to your teacher pronounce the sentences in the chart above.

EXERCISE 1 Fill in the blanks with the affirmative of the verb given. Use the future with *be going to*. Use contractions when possible.

1. Shafia <u>'s going to get</u> some things for the baby.
   get

2. Halina and Dorota _____ Shafia again on Thursday.
   see

3. Shafia's mother _____ her with the new baby.
   help

4. The new baby _____ soon.

arrive

5. Shafia's relatives _____ a lot of gifts for the baby.

bring

6. Halina and Dorota _____ Shafia to the resale shop.

take

7. Shafia _____ a stroller for the baby.

need

8. Shafia and Ali _____ parents for the first time.

be

9. With the help of her friends, Shafia _____ ready for the baby.

be

10. Shafia's mother _____ her daughter for a month.

visit

11. Shafia and Ali _____ their new baby.

enjoy

9.2 The Future—Negative Statements

Subject	Be + Not	Going To	Verb (Base Form)	
I	am not	going to	need	a new car seat.
Shafia's father	is not	going to	visit	her in January.
We	are not	going to	buy	a lot of things.
You	are not	going to	give	us a stroller.
Shafia's relatives	are not	going to	come	to the resale shop on Thursday.
There	are not	going to	be	many people at the resale shop.

EXERCISE 2 Fill in the blanks with the negative form of *be going to*. Use the verbs given. Use contractions when possible.

1. Shafia ___isn't going to buy___ a lot of baby clothes.

buy

2. With a new baby, Shafia and Ali _____ a lot of sleep.

get

3. Shafia's mother _____ for a year.

stay

4. Shafia _____ a lot of sleep for a while.

get

5. Dorota, Halina, and Shafia _____ at the resale store today.

shop

6. There _____ enough space in Dorota's car for the baby furniture.

be

7. Relatives _____ Shafia a crib.

give

8. The resale shop _____ open next Sunday.

be

9. Dorota and Halina _____ any baby clothes at the resale shop.

buy

10. Ali _____ Shafia to the resale shop.

take

9.3 The Future—Use

Examples	Explanation
Shafia**'s going to buy** some things for the baby.	We use *be going to* with future plans.
You**'re not going to get** much sleep.	We use *be going to* with predictions for the future.

Language Note:

We often shorten *going to go* to *going*.

We're **going to go** to the resale shop next week. = We're **going** to the resale shop next week.

EXERCISE 3 Fill in the blanks with the affirmative or negative form of *be going to* and the verb given. Use contractions when possible.

Shafia and Ali _____*are going to be*_____ parents very soon. They're excited, but a
                        1. be

little worried. Things _____*aren't going to be*_____ the same. There
                        2. not/be

_____ many changes. The baby _____ in two
      3. be   **4. arrive**

months. Then, Ali _____ two weeks off from work. He
                        5. take

_____ able to take off any more time because he has a new job.
      6. not/be

Shafia's mother _____ for a month to help. She
                 7. come

_____ so Shafia can take care of the baby. Shafia and Ali
      8. cook and clean

_____ a lot of new things before the baby comes. For example, they
      9. buy

need a crib, a high chair, and a stroller. They _____ a lot of money
                               10. not/have

after the baby arrives. Shafia _____ to English classes for a while, but
                       11. not/go

both Shafia and Ali _____ a special class for new parents at the
                 12. take

community center.

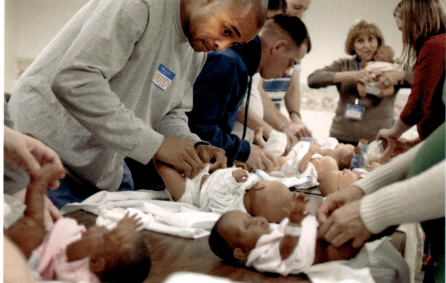

9.4 Time Expressions

Time expressions can go at the beginning or end of the sentence. Learn the prepositions with each time expression.

Examples	Explanation
She's going to visit me **in two weeks**. **In January**, he's going to visit me. They're going to visit me **in 2020**.	We use *in* with numbers of days, weeks, months, or years in the future. It means *after*. We use *in* with years or names of months.
I'm going to visit you **on January 12**.	We use *on* with dates.
On Thursday, I'm going shopping. I'm going shopping **this Thursday**.	We use *on* or *this* with names of days. *This* means a future day in a present week.
This week, I'm going to get some new clothes. My parents are going to visit **next week**.	We use *this* with future time in the same week, month, or year. We use *next* with future time after the present week.
Tomorrow I'm going to help you. I'm not going to help you **tonight**.	We use *tomorrow* for the day after today. *Tonight* means this night.
She's going to stay with us **for a while**.	*For a while* means for an indefinite amount of time.
She's going to live here **for a year**.	We use *for* with a time period.
We're going to see our relatives **soon**.	We use *soon* for a near future time that is not specific.
Ali's going to come home from work **at 6:00 p.m.**	We use *at* for a specific time in the future.

EXERCISE 4 Fill in the blanks with the correct preposition for each time expression. Use *in*, *on*, *at*, and *for*.

1. Shafia's going to have her baby _____ *in* _____ two months.

2. Shafia's going to visit the resale shop _____ Thursday.

3. Shafia and Ali are going to stay in their apartment _____ a while.

4. Ali's going to be home _____ 6:00 p.m. tonight.

5. Ali's life is going to change a lot _____ November.

6. Shafia's mother is going to stay with her _____ a month.

7. Shafia's mother is going to arrive _____ November 10.

8. Shafia and Ali's child is going to be in school _____ 2020.

EXERCISE 5 About You Make predictions about your future. Think about your life in ten years. Use the verbs given in the affirmative or negative with *be going to*. Add more information where possible.

1. live in an apartment

   In ten years, I'm not going to live in an apartment.

   I'm going to have a house.

2. live in this city

   _____

   _____

3. be a student

   _____

   _____

4. work in an office

   _____

   _____

5. have a big family

   _____

   _____

6. be a U.S. citizen

   _____

   _____

7. forget my language

   _____

   _____

8. return to my country to live

   _____

   _____

9. have a car OR have a different car

   _____

   _____

EXERCISE 6 Look at part of Shafia's calendar. Write about her activities. Make affirmative and/or negative statements with *be going to* and the words given. Add a time expression in the future. Then rewrite the sentence with a different time expression. Use the expressions on page 203.

		SEPTEMBER		
MONDAY	**TUESDAY**	**WEDNESDAY**	**THURSDAY**	**FRIDAY**
1 TODAY Errands 10 a.m. to 1 p.m.	2 Exercise class 9 a.m. to 11 a.m.	3	4 Resale shop 1 p.m.	5
8	9 Doctor's appointment 3 p.m.	10	11	12 Visit Ali's parents
15 Errands 10 a.m. to 1 p.m.	16 Exercise class 9 a.m. to 11 a.m.	17	18	19 Dinner with Ali, Halina and Peter 7 p.m.
22	23 Doctor's appointment 3 p.m.	24	25 Get ready for the trip to New York—Ali	26 Movie at home with Dorota—Ali out of town

1. Shafia/be busy

   Shafia's going to be busy this month.

   She isn't going to go shopping tomorrow.

2. Ali/be out of town

   _____

   _____

3. Shafia/take an exercise class

   _____

   _____

4. Dorota/come to Shafia's house

   _____

   _____

continued

5. Shafia/see the doctor

_____

_____

6. Ali/get ready for a trip to New York

_____

_____

7. Shafia, Halina, and Dorota/go to the resale shop

_____

_____

8. Shafia and Ali/have dinner with Halina and Peter

_____

_____

9. Shafia and Ali/visit Ali's parents

_____

_____

10. Shafia/have free time

_____

_____

11. Shafia/run errands

_____

_____

EXERCISE 7 Complete the conversations. Use the verbs given in the affirmative or negative with _be going to_. Use contractions when possible.

CD 2
TR 23

CONVERSATION A: Halina and Shafia are talking about the new baby's room.

Halina: Where's the baby's room?

Shafia: We have an extra room. It's small. But there _'s going to be_ _____ enough
                                                                      1. be

space for a crib.

Halina: What's in the room now?

Shafia: There's a desk and a computer. But we _____ them there. Ali
2. leave

_____ them to the living room next week. His brother
3. move

_____ him. The desk is very heavy.
4. help

Halina: What about the color of the walls?

Shafia: We _____ them yellow. But not now. There
5. paint

_____ enough time.
6. be

CONVERSATION B: Halina, Dorota, and Shafia are talking about the baby's name.

Halina: Shafia, do you have a name for the baby?

Shafia: No. Ali and I _____ a name right now. After the baby's birth,
7. choose

we _____ some of our relatives for ideas. It's very important to choose
8. ask

the right name.

Dorota: There are long lists of names on the Internet. Just search for[1] *baby names*. You can even find the

meaning of each name.

Shafia: That's interesting. But the baby _____ an American name.
9. have

We _____ the baby a name from our country.
10. give

Dorota: There are names from other countries online too. There are thousands of names for boys and girls.

Shafia: Thanks, Dorota. But we _____ to
11. wait

see the baby first.

> *Dorota* means gift from God. *Halina* means light. *Shafia* means mercy.

_____

[1] *Search for* means look for.

2

GRAMMAR

The Future—*Yes/No* Questions

The Future—*Wh-* Questions

The Future—Questions with *How Long*

The Future— Subject Questions

CONTEXT

Moving

A woman packs a box of kitchen items.

BEFORE YOU READ

1. Is it hard to move? Why or why not?

2. How do people prepare to move?

READ

CD 2
TR 24

Read the following conversation. Pay special attention to *yes/no* questions and *wh-* questions with *be going to* in bold.

DID YOU KNOW?
Common reasons for moving are family-related, employment-related, and housing-related.

Victor and Simon are on the phone. Victor and his family are moving soon. Simon is giving him some advice.

Victor: We're going to move in two weeks. There's so much to do!

Simon: You're right. **Are you going to hire** a mover?

Victor: No, I'm not. I'm going to rent a truck. The new apartment is in our neighborhood. Lisa and I don't have a lot of things. But we're going to need some help. **Are** you **going to be** available on the 27th of this month?

Simon: Sure. I can help you.

Victor: Thanks, Simon. What should I do about our mail?

Simon: You can fill out a change-of-address form at the post office. Or you can fill it out online. It's easy! The post office sends your mail to your new address for one year.

Victor: What else do we need to do?

Simon: **Are you going to get** Internet service in your new apartment?

Victor: We're going to need a wireless Internet service I think.

Simon: Then you can call and make an appointment. The company can come and set it up. They often have cheap rates if you get phone, Internet, and TV together. This is a package.

Victor: That sounds like a good deal. **How long is it going to take** for the new service?

Simon: You can make an appointment for the day after you move in. They can usually set it up within an hour or so.

Victor: Oh, great.

Simon: **When are you going to pack? Are you going to need** boxes?

Victor: I'm starting to pack now. We have some boxes, but not enough.

Simon: You should go to some stores in your neighborhood. You can ask them for their old boxes.

Victor: That's a good idea. We also have a lot of old things. **What are we going to do** with them? I don't want to move them.

Simon: You can give them to charity. There's a resale shop in this neighborhood.

OFFICIAL MAIL FORWARDING CHANGE OF ADDRESS ORDER

OFFICIAL USE ONLY
Zone/Route ID No.

Please PRINT items 1-10 in blue or black ink. Your signature is required in item 9.

1. Change of Address for: (Read Attached Instructions)	2. Is This Move Temporary?		

☐ Individual (#5) ☐ Entire Family (#5) ☐ Business (#6)   ☐ Yes   ☐ No

Date Entered on Form 3982
M M   D D   Y   Y

4. If TEMPORARY move, print date to discontinue forwarding: (ex. 03/27/05)

3. Start Date: (ex. 02/27/05)

Expiration Date
M M   D D   Y   Y

5a. LAST Name & Jr./Sr./etc.

Clerk/Carrier Endorsement

5b.FIRST Name and MI

6. If BUSINESS

...MBER AND STREET NAME (INCLUDE ST., AVE., CT., ETC.) OR PO BOX

Vocabulary	Context
move	We're going to **move** to a new apartment in two weeks.
hire	The school needs a new English teacher. The school is going to **hire** a new teacher.
mover	We need a **mover** to help us with the furniture.
rent	I can **rent** a truck for one day. It's not expensive.
truck	The car isn't big enough. You're going to need a **truck**.
neighborhood	Victor and Lisa are moving close to their old apartment. Their new apartment is in the same **neighborhood**.
address	They live on Madison Street. Their **address** is 1245 Madison Street.
wireless	I have **wireless** Internet service at home. I don't need any cords to get online.
package	I am going to order a **package**. It comes with different services.
pack	I'm going to **pack** my things. I'm going to put them in boxes.

LISTEN

CD 2
TR 25

Listen to the sentences about the conversation. Circle *true* or *false*.

1. (True)	False	5. True	False
2. True	False	6. True	False
3. True	False	7. True	False
4. True	False	8. True	False

9.5 The Future—*Yes/No* Questions

PART A

Be	Subject	*Going To*	Verb (Base Form)		Short Answer
Am	I	**going to**	**need**	a change-of-address form?	Yes, you are.
Are	you	**going to**	**get**	Internet service?	Yes, you are.
Is	Victor	**going to**	**move**	to another city?	No, he isn't.
Are	we	**going to**	**give**	our old items to charity?	We, we are.
Are	Victor and Lisa	**going to**	**hire**	a mover?	No, they aren't.
Are	there	**going to**	**be**	any problems?	No, there aren't.

PART B Compare the word order in statements and yes/no questions:

Statements	Yes/No Questions
You are going to move.	**Are you** going to move to a new neighborhood?
I am going to need a truck.	**Am I** going to need boxes?

EXERCISE 1 Write *yes/no* questions about Victor and Simon's conversation on page 209. Use *be going to* and the words given. Give a short answer.

1. Victor's family/move soon

   <u>Is Victor's family going to move soon? Yes, they are.</u>

2. Victor/hire a mover

   _____

3. he/buy some boxes

   _____

4. their new apartment/be in the same neighborhood

   _____

5. he/get Internet service

   _____

6. it/take a long time to get Internet service

   _____

7. the post office/send Victor and Lisa's mail to their new address

   _____

8. Victor/have to pay for boxes

   _____

9. they/move all their things to their new apartment

   _____

EXERCISE 2 Complete the short conversations. Write a *yes/no* question with *be going to*. Use the words given.

1. **A:** We're going to move.

   B: <u>Are you going to move this week?</u>
   _____
   this week

2. **A:** I'm going to change my address.

   B: _____
   your phone number too

3. **A:** He's going to pay for that service.

   B: _____
   more than $50

continued

4. **A:** They're going to move.

   B: _____
   to a house

5. **A:** Simon's going to help.

   B: _____
   Marta too

6. **A:** They're not going to move all their things.

   B: _____
   give some things to charity

7. **A:** Victor and Lisa are going to rent a new apartment.

   B: _____
   in a different city

8. **A:** Victor's going to get a change-of-address form.

   B: _____
   online

9.6 The Future—*Wh-* Questions

Question Word(s)	Be	Subject	*Going To*	Verb (Base Form)		Short Answer
Why	**are**	you	**going to**	**move?**		Because my apartment is too small.
Where	**are**	Victor and Lisa	**going to**	**live?**		In the same neighborhood.
What	**is**	he	**going to**	**give**	to charity?	Their old things.
When	**are**	they	**going to**	**get**	boxes?	Next week.
How many boxes	**are**	they	**going to**	**get?**		About 50.
What kind of truck	**is**	he	**going to**	**rent?**		A big one.
What kinds of supplies	**are**	you	**going to**	**buy**	at the store?	A pad of paper, pens, and pencils.

Language Notes:

1. Remember, some question words can contract with *is*.

   Where's Victor going to live?   **Why's** he going to move?

2. In answers to *wh-* questions, use a pronoun. We don't repeat the nouns.

PART B Compare the word order in statements and *wh-* questions:

Statements	*Wh-* Questions
You are going to move.	When **are you** going to move?
I am going to need boxes.	How many boxes **am I** going to need?

EXERCISE 3 Ask a *wh-* question about each statement. Use *going to* and the question words given.

1. **A:** Victor's going to get a change-of-address form.

   B: Where's he going to get it?
   where

2. **A:** I'm going to rent a truck.

   B: _____
   when

3. **A:** Victor's going to go to stores in his neighborhood.

   B: _____
   why

4. **A:** There are going to be some problems.

   B: _____
   what kind of

5. **A:** I'm going to move this furniture to my new apartment.

   B: _____
   how

6. **A:** You're going to need boxes.

   B: _____
   how many

7. **A:** The truck is going to cost money.

   B: _____
   how much

8. **A:** I'm going to give some items to charity.

   B: _____
   which

9. **A:** We're going to get some boxes.

   B: _____
   where

EXERCISE 4 Complete the conversations. Look at the short answer to each question. Then ask a question with the words given. Use the correct question word with *be going to*.

1. **A:** When's Victor going to move?
   Victor/move

   B: In about two weeks.

2. **A:** _____
   Victor and Lisa/rent

   B: A truck.

3. **A:** _____
   the cost/be for new Internet service

   B: Less than $100.

continued

4. A: _____
they/move

B: Because their apartment is too small.

5. A: _____
Simon/help Victor

B: On the 25th of this month.

6. A: _____
Victor/get boxes

B: From a store in the neighborhood.

7. A: _____
Victor and Lisa/rent

B: A large, three-bedroom apartment.

8. A: _____
Victor and Lisa/pack

B: 50 boxes.

9. A: _____
Victor/do

B: Give them to charity.

10. A: _____
the phone company/change your service

B: On moving day.

11. A: _____
you/have the same phone number

B: Because I'm going to live in the same neighborhood.

9.7 The Future—Questions with *How Long*

Examples	Explanation
A: How long are you going to stay? **B: Until** next week.	We use *how long* to ask about specific amounts of time. We can use *until* in answers to *how long* questions. Use *until* when the action ends at a specific time.
A: How long are they going to wait? **B: For** 15 minutes.	We can use *for* in answers to *how long* questions. Use *for* when the action takes an amount of time.

EXERCISE 5 About You Find a partner. Use the words given to ask questions with *how long* and *be going to*. Your partner can give an answer with *for* or *until*. Write the questions and answers for practice.

1. you/be in this class

   A: How long are you going to be in this class?

   B: I'm going to be in this class until the end of the semester.

2. our class/work on this exercise

   A: _____

   B: _____

3. we/use this book

   A: _____

   B: _____

4. you/stay at school today

   A: _____

   B: _____

5. this school/be open today

   A: _____

   B: _____

6. you/be a student

   A: _____

   B: _____

continued

7. you/stay in the United States

A: _____

B: _____

9.8 The Future—Subject Questions

Question Word(s)	Be	Going To	Verb (Base Form)		Answer
What	is	going to	happen?		I'm going to move.
Who	is	going to	help	you?	My friends are.
How many friends	are	going to	help	you?	Four.
Which services	are	going to	come	with the package?	Phone, Internet, and TV.

EXERCISE 6 Write a subject question for each statement. Use *going to* and the question word(s) given. Use contractions when possible.

1. Somebody's going to visit me.

   Who's going to visit you?
   _____
   who

2. Something's going to change.

   _____
   what

3. Many people are going to move this year.

   _____
   how many

4. Some services are going to be expensive.

   _____
   which

5. Somebody's going to give me some boxes.

   _____
   who

6. Something's going to happen on Thursday.

   _____
   what

7. A mover's going to help me.

   _____
   which

8. Some apartments are going to be available.

   _____
   how many

EXERCISE 7 Victor is calling a truck rental company. He wants to rent a truck for his move. Complete Victor's conversation using *yes/no* questions and *wh-* questions with *be going to*. Use the words given.

Employee: Avery Truck Rental. How can I help you?

Victor: I need to rent a truck. I'm going to move, and I need some information about prices.

Employee: Sure. __Are you going to return__ the truck here or in another city?
                            1. you/return

Victor: I'm going to return it here.

Employee: OK. _____?
                            2. what kind of truck/you/need

Victor: Uh … I don't know.

Employee: Well, _____?
                            3. how many rooms/you/move

Victor: It's a two-bedroom apartment.

Employee: A 15-foot truck is enough.

Victor: _____?
                            4. it/have/room for my sofa

Employee: Oh, yes. It's going to be fine. _____?
                            5. when/you/move

Victor: In two weeks.

Employee: _____ on the weekend or during the week?
                            6. it/be

Victor: I'm not sure. Why is that important?

Employee: It's $20 a day more on the weekend. And we don't have many trucks available on the weekends.

Victor: _____ any trucks available two weeks from today?
                            7. there/be

Employee: _____ enough?
                            8. one day/be

Victor: Yes. I need it for just one day.

Employee: OK. It's going to be $49.99 a day and 99 cents a mile. I need a credit card number to reserve

           it. _____?
                            9. what kind of card/you/use

Victor: I'm not ready to reserve it now. I'm only calling about prices. Thank you.

EXERCISE 8 Complete the conversation between Victor and Simon. Use the phrases from the box.

are going to help	I'm going to invite	aren't going to move	We're going to meet
I'm going to get	are you going to pack ✓	are you going to be	

Simon: When _____*are you going to pack*_____ the rest of your things?
                              1.

Victor: This week. _____ more boxes today.
                              2.

Simon: Ed and I can help you move on Saturday, the 27th. We're available all day.

Victor: Thanks, but the people in my new apartment _____ until
                                                              3.

Sunday. _____ available on Sunday?
               4.

Simon: I think so. How many people _____ you?
                                        5.

Victor: Just two of my friends. _____ at my apartment at 1:00.
                                    6.

Then later, _____ you all for pizza.
                7.

EXERCISE 9 Read the following blog. Complete the blog using the correct form of *be going to* and *yes/no* questions and *wh-* questions with *be going to* and the the verbs given. Use contractions when possible.

Moving FAQs

1. When is the best time to move?

   That depends. May through September _____ are going to be _____ the busiest
                                      a. be

   months for moving companies. _____ yourself, or are you
                                          b. move

   going to hire a mover? Either way, it _____ easier in the
                                           c. be

   off-season.

2. How long _____ to get ready?
                          a. take

   For most people, it _____ 6–8 weeks to do everything. Start
                               b. take

   planning early. If you wait, you _____ enough time.
                                  c. not/have

3. How much _____?
                         a. cost

   It _____ more if you hire movers and if you have a lot of stuff.
                   b. cost

   A moving company _____ someone to your house about
                             c. send

   4 weeks before the move. They _____ at how much stuff you
                                 d. look

   have and give you a price.

4. What should I do before the moving company comes?

   Get rid of everything you _____ with you to your new home.
                                 a. not/take

   You _____ it. Give it to a charity or throw it away.
                   b. not/want

WRITING

PART 1 Editing Advice

1. Use a form of *be* with *going to*.

   We <u>*'re*</u> going to shop at a resale shop.

2. Use the correct word order in questions.

   Where <u>*are they*</u> ~~they are~~ going to work?

3. Use the correct preposition with time expressions.

   We are going to move <u>*in*</u> ~~after~~ two weeks.

4. Don't forget *to* after *going*.

   Victor's going <u>*to*</u> rent a truck.

5. Don't forget the *-ing* on *going to*.

   I'm <u>*going*</u> ~~go~~ to move next week.

PART 2 Editing Practice

Some of the shaded words and phrases have mistakes. Find the mistakes and correct them.
If the shaded words are correct, write *C*.

Dorota: We <u>*'re*</u> going to have a party for Shafia. It's going to be <u>*C*</u> at my house. Can you help me?
1.   2.

Halina: Sure. What kind of party are you go to have?
3.

Dorota: A baby shower.

Halina: A baby shower? What's that?

Dorota: At a baby shower, people have lunch together. And everyone brings a gift for the baby.

Halina: When it's going to be?
4.

Dorota: The party going to be next weekend, on Saturday, the 13th.
5.   6.

Halina: Who's going be there?
7.

Dorota: Shafia's relatives and good friends.

Halina: Are we going to cook?
8.

Dorota: We're going to cook some things. But we're go to buy prepared food at the deli too.
9.   10.

I'm going order a cake too!
11.

Halina: What time the party going to start?
12.

Dorota: In 2 p.m.
13.

Halina: But Peter has to work until 4 p.m. on Saturday.
14.

Dorota: Don't worry. This shower's for women only.

PART 3 Write About It

Write a paragraph of six to eight sentences about the picture. Write about what is happening right now and what is going to happen.

Victor is coming out of his apartment building. He is moving today.

PART 4 Learner's Log

1. Write one sentence about each of the topics:
   - Preparing for a new baby
   - Resale shops
   - Preparing to move
   - Renting a truck

2. Write any questions you still have about each topic above.

Choices

Schoolboys watch their
classmates play chess.

I am who I am today because of
the choices I made yesterday.

— Eleanor Roosevelt

1

GRAMMAR

Comparative Forms of
Adjectives

Spelling of the *-er* Form

Comparisons with Nouns
and Verbs

CONTEXT

Higher Education

BEFORE YOU READ

1. Where is the state university in your state?

2. What community colleges do you know about in your area?

CD 2
TR 28

READ

Read the following article. Pay special attention to comparative forms in bold.

In the United States, many students choose to go to a community college. Students can get a two-year certificate or degree. Some students start their education at a community college. Then they go to a four-year college or university to get a bachelor's degree.

A four-year university is **more expensive than** a community college. The average tuition at a community college is $3,264 a year. At a four-year state university, it's $8,893 a year.[1] A community college is often **closer** to home **than** a four-year college. Community colleges in big cities often have several campuses.

There are other differences too. A community college often has **smaller classes than** a university. Some university classes can have **more than** 100 students. Also, students at a community college are usually **older than** students at a four-year college. The average age of students at a community college is 29. At a university, most students are between the ages of 18 and 24.

Community college students are often **busier** too. Many students have full- or part-time jobs and families. Community colleges are **more convenient than** universities for students with small children. Many community colleges offer child care. There are more night and weekend classes too.

Which is **better** for you: a community college or a four-year college?

_____
[1] These statistics are from 2013–2014.

> **DID YOU KNOW?**
> There are different levels of college degrees: associate's degree, bachelor's degree, master's degree, and PhD (or doctorate).

Vocabulary	Context
certificate	My cousin has a **certificate** from a community college to work with children.
education	We go to school to get an **education**.
bachelor's degree	My brother has a **degree** from a four-year college. He has a **bachelor's degree** in political science.
average	I'm 22, my brother is 23, and my sister is 27. Our **average** age is 24.
tuition	College is not free. Students have to pay **tuition** to go to college.
campus	My college has several **campuses**. There is a **campus** near my house. There is a **campus** downtown too.
between	The number 20 is **between** 19 and 21.
offer	The college **offers** good services for students. It has child care and weekend classes.
child care	People with small children need **child care** when they work or go to school. It is sometimes called day care.

Listen to the sentences about the article. Circle *true* or *false*.

CD 2
TR 29

1. (True)	False	5. True	False
2. True	False	6. True	False
3. True	False	7. True	False
4. True	False	8. True	False

10.1 Comparative Forms of Adjectives

We can compare two people or things.

Simple Form	Comparative Form	Examples	Explanation
old tall	old**er** tall**er**	Community college students are **older than** university students.	After a one-syllable adjective, we add -er.
busy happy	bus**ier** happ**ier**	Community college students are often **busier than** university students.	After a two-syllable adjective that ends in y, we change the y to an i and add -er.
simple quiet friendly	simpl**er**, **more** simple quiet**er**, **more** quiet friendl**ier**, **more** friendly	My new neighborhood is **quieter than** my old one. My new neighborhood is **more quiet than** my old one.	Some two-syllable adjectives have two forms.
helpful crowded expensive flexible	**more** helpful **more** crowded **more** expensive **more** flexible	University tuition is **more expensive than** community college tuition. Online classes are **more flexible than** regular classes.	With most other two-syllable adjectives and all three-syllable adjectives, we add *more* before the adjective.
good bad	**better** **worse**	The movie *Star Wars* is **better than** *Star Trek*. A bad grade is **worse than** a good grade.	Some comparative forms are irregular. We change the word completely.

Language Notes:

1. We use *than* to complete the comparison. We omit *than* if we do not mention the second item of comparison.

   The university is **bigger than** the college, but the college is **more convenient**.

2. We can put *much* before a comparative form.

   Those students are **much younger** than we are.

3. It is very formal to use the subject pronoun after *than*. Most Americans use the object pronoun.

   Formal: You are busier than **I** am.

   Informal: You are busier than **me**.

10.2 Spelling of the -er Form

Simple Adjective	Comparative Adjective	Explanation
old cheap	old**er** cheap**er**	We add -er to most adjectives.
big hot	big**ger** hot**ter**	If a one-syllable adjective ends with consonant + vowel + consonant, we double the final consonant before adding -er.
nice late	nice**r** late**r**	If the adjective ends in e, we add -r only.
busy easy	bus**ier** eas**ier**	If a two-syllable adjective ends in y, we change the y to i and add -er.

EXERCISE 1 Write the comparative forms of the adjectives. Use correct spelling with -er endings. In some cases, there are two answers.

1. busy _____busier_____

2. excited _____more excited_____

3. friendly __friendlier OR more friendly__

4. convenient _____

5. big _____

6. fine _____

7. lazy _____

8. hard _____

9. funny _____

10. expensive _____

11. large _____

12. interesting _____

13. quiet _____

14. hot _____

15. good _____

16. kind _____

17. mad _____

18. late _____

19. bad _____

20. cheap _____

21. simple _____

22. long _____

23. beautiful _____

24. cold _____

25. small _____

26. angry _____

27. boring _____

28. healthy _____

EXERCISE 2 Compare Wilson Community College and Jackson University using the information in the table. Fill in the blanks with the comparative form of one of the adjectives from the box. Add *than* where necessary. The numbers in the table go with the numbers in the exercise.

	Wilson Community College	Jackson University
1.	night and weekend classes	no night or weekend classes
2.	$90 per credit hour[2]	$450 per credit hour
3.	average class size = 16 students	average class size = 30 students
4.	80 percent of students have jobs	10 percent of students have jobs
5.	child care	no child care
6.	all classes in one building	more than 60 buildings
7.	opened in 1985	opened in 1910
8.	good for me	good for my sister

busy   good   big   flexible✓   old   small   expensive   convenient

1. Wilson is ___ more flexible than ___ Jackson for people with day jobs.

2. Jackson is _____ Wilson.

3. Classes at Wilson are _____ classes at Jackson.

4. Most students at Wilson work full-time. Students at Wilson are _____

   students at Jackson.

5. Wilson is _____ Jackson for parents with small children.

6. Jackson is _____ Wilson.

7. Jackson is _____ Wilson.

8. Wilson is good for me, but Jackson is _____ for my sister because she's

   finishing her bachelor's degree.

_____

[2] College students get credits for their classes. The number of credits usually
depends on the number of hours of class per week. For a three-hour course,
a student gets three credits.

EXERCISE 3 Use the comparative form of the adjectives from the boxes to fill in the blanks. Add *than* where necessary.

convenient	close	cheap ✓	old	busy	young

CONVERSATION 1

A: I don't plan to go to Cassidy University. I prefer Central Community College.

B: Why?

A: The tuition's only $1,800 a semester. It's _____ *cheaper* _____ than a four-year college.
1.

Also it's _____ to my home, so I can walk there. And the students are
2.

_____. I'm 32. A lot of the students are in their 30s and 40s.
3.

B: You're right. Most of the students at Cassidy are _____ the students at
4.

Central. They're under 22 years old.

CONVERSATION 2

A: A lot of the community college students have small children. Central has child care. So it's

_____ for people with small children.
5.

B: You don't have kids.

A: No. But my sister does. We're planning to take classes together. She has a full-time job. Her kids are

young. So she's much _____ I am. The child care is really great for her.
6.

expensive	slow	bad	hard	convenient	interesting	cheap	good

CONVERSATION 3

A: I prefer Cassidy University.

B: Why? The tuition is high. Cassidy is _____ Central.
7.

A: I know. But I want to be a nurse, and Cassidy's nursing program is _____
8.

Central's nursing program. I can save money with my textbooks. I can buy them online. They're

_____ online than at the bookstore.
9.

B: But it's _____ to buy your books online. Sometimes it takes a week.
10.

A: Yes, but it's _____. The books come right to my house.
11.

continued

CONVERSATION 4

A: I'm having a problem with my grades. My classes this semester are _____

12.

my classes last semester. And my grades are not so good. My grades this semester are

_____ my grades last semester.

13.

B: You should go to your teachers for help.

A: You're right. How are your classes this semester?

B: I love my history class, but my math class is just numbers. It's boring. My history class is

_____ my math class.

14.

EXERCISE 4 About You Compare yourself to another person.

1. tall

   I am taller than my best friend. OR My brother is taller than me.

2. responsible

   _____

3. helpful

   _____

4. busy

   _____

5. funny

   _____

6. friendly

   _____

7. polite

   _____

8. strong

   _____

9. quiet

   _____

10.3 Comparisons with Nouns and Verbs

Examples	Explanation
Part-time students need **more time** to finish college **than** full-time students do.	We can use *more* before nouns to make a comparison statement. Use *than* before the second item of comparison.
You spend **less money** at a community college than at a university. My math class has **fewer students** than my biology class.	We can use *less* or *fewer* with nouns to make a comparison: • Use *less* with noncount nouns. • Use *fewer* with count nouns.
I prefer the city college because it costs **less**. You pay much **more** at a university. I study **harder** on the weekends.	We can use a comparative form after verbs.

EXERCISE 5 About You Find a partner. Tell your partner about yourself using the words given. Then write sentences about you and your partner.

1. have books

   I have more books than Jalilah.

2. work hard

   _____

3. take classes

   _____

4. walk

   _____

5. have time to relax

   _____

6. study

   _____

7. have brothers and sisters

   _____

8. exercise

   _____

EXERCISE 6 Compare Central Community College and Cassidy University using the information in the table. Add *than* where necessary. The numbers in the table go with the numbers in the exercise.

	Central Community College	Cassidy University
1. students	2,000	10,000
2. cost per credit hour	$120	$250
3. night classes	150	50
4. books in library	8,000	50,000
5. campuses	5	2
6. average number of students in a class	16	30
7. students over the age of 40	215	77
8. married students	800	200

1. Cassidy has __more students than__ Central.

2. Central costs _____ per credit hour.

3. Central has _____ Cassidy.

4. Central has _____ in its library.

5. Central has _____ Cassidy.

6. Central has _____ in a class.

7. Central has _____ over the age of 40.

8. Cassidy has _____ Central.

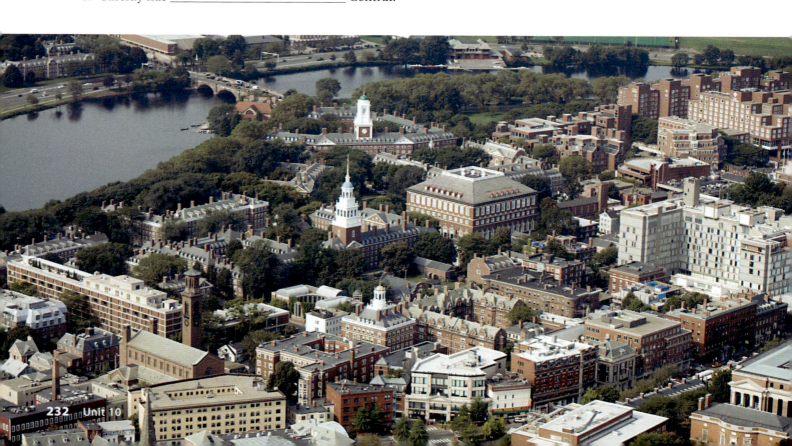

EXERCISE 7 Read the article. Complete the sentences with comparative forms.

College is a big change for many students. In high school, there is _____
1.
homework, but students often spend _____ time in class. Students in college are
2.
sometimes only in classes for three hours a day, while high school students are in classes six or seven

hours. In college, students study _____ outside of class. They often spend as
3.
much as four hours in the library. Another difference is the size of the classes. High schools classes often

have _____ students, maybe 20–25 in each class. In college, some classes are
4.
small, but most classes are much _____. Sometimes there are as many as 200
5.
students! College students have _____ freedom, but they also have
6.
_____ work and _____ stress. They are often
7.   8.
_____ worried than high school students, and sleep
9.
_____ than high school students do.
10.

2

GRAMMAR

Superlative Forms of
  Adjectives

Spelling of the *-est* Form

Superlatives with Nouns
  and Verbs

CONTEXT

Buying a Car

There are different cars to choose from.

BEFORE YOU READ

1. Do you have a car? Is it a new car or a used car? What kind of car is it?

2. What's your favorite car? Why?

READ

CD 2
TR 31

Read the following conversation. Pay special attention to superlative forms in bold.

Victor: I want to buy a used car. My coworker, Sam, wants to sell me his 2010 car. He wants $6,000. Is that a good price?

Simon: I don't know. **The best way** to get information about used car prices is in the *blue book*.

Victor: What's the *blue book*?

Simon: The *blue book* shows prices and other information about new and used cars. It can help you. We can look at it online. Then you can make a decision.

(after Simon goes online)

Simon: Look. Here's your coworker's car.

Victor: There are three prices for the same car. Why?

Simon: The price depends on several things: condition of the car, mileage, and extras, like heated seats and hands-free phone systems. Cars in **the best condition** with **the lowest mileage** and **the most extras** are **the most expensive**. Cars with **the highest mileage** and **the most problems** are **the cheapest**.

Victor: Sam says his car is in good condition.

Simon: **The best way** to know for sure is to take it to a mechanic. You need a good car. Repairs are very expensive.

Victor: But it costs money to go to a mechanic.

Simon: It's better to lose $300 than $6,000. But the price of the car is not the only thing to consider. Also look at fuel economy. There's a website that compares fuel economy. Here it is. Look. Your coworker's car gets only 19 miles per gallon.[3] Look at these other two cars. This car gets 30 miles per gallon. This one gets 35 miles per gallon. Your coworker's car is **the cheapest** to buy but it isn't **the most economical** to use.

Victor: There's a lot to know about buying a used car!

---

[3] An abbreviation for *miles per gallon* is mpg.

DID YOU KNOW?
When you buy a new or used car, you do not always have to pay the asking price. The buyer can try to get a lower price from the seller.

Vocabulary	Context
coworker	Victor works with Sam. Sam is Victor's **coworker**.
make a decision	There are many choices. Victor has to **make a decision**.
depend on	The price of the car **depends on** miles, condition, etc.
condition	My car is in good **condition**. I have no problems with it.
mileage	How many miles does the car have? What is its **mileage**?
extras	This model has a lot of **extras**. It has heated seats, a remote starter, and a hands-free phone.
like	My car has extras, **like** heated seats.
mechanic	A **mechanic** fixes cars.
repair	An old car needs a lot of **repairs**.
consider	You have to **consider** a lot of things before you buy a car.
fuel economy	This car doesn't use a lot of gas. This car has good **fuel economy**.
economical	It is very **economical**. It isn't expensive and it's good quality.

LISTEN

Listen to the sentences about the conversation. Circle *true* or *false*.

1. True   (False)   5. True   False

2. True   False   6. True   False

3. True   False   7. True   False

4. True   False   8. True   False

10.4 Superlative Forms of Adjectives

We use the superlative form to point out the number one item in a group of three or more. We add *the* before the superlative form.

Simple Form	Superlative Form	Examples	Explanation
low tall	**the** low**est** **the** tall**est**	Car A has **the lowest** mileage.	After a one-syllable adjective, we add *-est*.
easy happy	**the** eas**iest** **the** happ**iest**	**The easiest** way to compare prices is with the blue book.	After a two-syllable adjective that ends in *y*, we change the *y* to *i* and add *-est*.
simple quiet friendly	**the** simpl**est** **the most** simple **the** quiet**est** **the most** quiet **the** friendl**iest** **the most** friendly	Car A is **the most quiet**. Car A is **the quietest**.	Some two-syllable adjectives have two forms.
helpful expensive	**the most** helpful **the most** expensive	Car A is **the most expensive** car.	With most other two-syllable adjectives and all three-syllable adjectives, we add *the most* before the adjective.
good bad	**the best** **the worst**	Which car is in **the best** condition? Car C is in **the worst** condition.	Some superlative forms are irregular. We change the word completely.

Language Notes:

1. We often add a prepositional phrase after a superlative phrase.

   Your car is the oldest car **in the parking lot**.

2. You can use *one of the* before a superlative form. The noun after it is plural.

   The blue car **is one of the** worst cars in the parking lot.

3. Omit *the* after a possessive form.

   My best friend has a new car.

10.5 Spelling of the *-est* Form

Simple Adjective	Superlative Adjective	Explanation
old cheap	old**est** cheap**est**	We add *-est* to most adjectives.
big hot	big**gest** hot**test**	If the adjective ends with consonant + vowel + consonant, we double the final consonant before adding *-est*.
nice late	nice**st** late**st**	If the adjective ends in *e*, we add *-st* only.
busy easy	bus**iest** eas**iest**	If a two-syllable adjective ends in *y*, we change the *y* to an *i* and add *-est*.

EXERCISE 1 Write the superlative form of the adjectives. Use correct spelling with *-est* endings. In some cases, there are two answers.

1. interesting ____the most interesting____
2. early _____the earliest_____
3. convenient _____
4. big _____
5. fine _____
6. lazy _____
7. funny _____
8. expensive _____
9. friendly _____
10. quiet _____

11. hot _____
12. good _____
13. kind _____
14. mad _____
15. late _____
16. helpful _____
17. busy _____
18. beautiful _____
19. healthy _____
20. small _____

EXERCISE 2 Victor is comparing three cars. Write superlative sentences about these cars, using the information in the table and the adjectives from the box.

	Car A	Car B	Car C
cost	$4,000	$12,000	$10,000
size	big enough for four passengers	big enough for five passengers	big enough for six passengers
year	2005	2013	2010
mileage	28 mpg	25 mpg	20 mpg
condition	needs work	very good condition	average condition

expensive	big	economical	old	good	cheap✓	bad	new

1. Car A costs $4,000. It's _____the cheapest_____ .
2. Car B costs $12,000. It's _____ .
3. Car C is _____ inside.
4. Car A is from 2005. It's _____ .
5. Car B is from 2013. It's _____ .
6. Car A gets 28 miles per gallon. In terms of gas, it's _____ .
7. Car B is in very good condition. It's _____ .
8. Car A is in very bad condition. It's _____ .

EXERCISE 3 Fill in the blanks with the superlative form of one of the adjectives from the boxes.

CD 2
TR 33

big	hard	close	good	smart	convenient

PART A

1. *On the phone:*

Shafia: I need your help. I want to buy a car. This is one of _____the biggest_____ decisions of
   1.

my life. What's _____ car?
   2.

Dorota: I can't answer that question. It depends on your needs.

2. *At home:*

Marta: This is your last year of high school. Let's talk about college for you. I prefer Lake College for

you because it's _____ to home. It's _____
   3.   4.

because you can walk there.

Tina: But Lake College isn't very good. I want to go to _____ college here in
   5.

the United States. I want to be a doctor.

Marta: It takes many years to become a doctor. You have to go to medical school and then practice in a

hospital. You are choosing one of _____ professions.[4]
   6.

Tina: I know, but I really want to be a doctor. I'm _____ student in my
   7.

biology class.

hard	slow	early	economical	easy	fast	good	expensive

PART B

3. *At the college:*

Halina: Which English class should we take?

Shafia: How about[5] this one? It starts at 8:00 A.M. It's _____ class of the day.
   8.

Halina: I don't like morning classes. How about this one?

Shafia: No, no. Not that one! That teacher is _____ at the school.
   9.

4. *At the electronics store:*

Halina: I need to buy a new computer. My old computer is slow. I want to buy

_____

[4] A *profession* is a job for a person with a college degree.

[5] We use *how about* to offer a helpful idea.

continued

_____ one. How about this one?
10.

Peter: Yes, it's fast. But look at the price! It's _____ computer in the store!
11.

5. *At the post office:*

Halina: What's _____ way to send this package? I need to save money.
12.

Clerk: You can send it by third-class mail. But it's _____ way. It can take a
13.

week.

EXERCISE 4 About You Write about people in your family for each of these items. Use superlatives.

1. tall

   My brother Tim is the tallest person in our family.

2. helpful

   _____

3. beautiful

   _____

4. nice

   _____

5. interesting

   _____

6. serious

   _____

7. funny

   _____

8. old

   _____

9. young

   _____

10. good at sports

   _____

11. bad at sports

_____

12. busy

_____

10.6 Superlatives with Nouns and Verbs

Examples	Explanation
Which car uses **the most gas**?	We can use *the most* before nouns to make superlative statements.
I want to spend **the least money** possible. This car has **the fewest extras**.	We can use *the least* and *the fewest* before nouns: • Use *the least* with noncount nouns. • Use *the fewest* with count nouns.
Which car costs **the least**? Who drives **the best** in your family?	We can use a superlative form after verbs.

CD 2 TR 34 **EXERCISE 5** Victor and Simon are looking at car prices online. Fill in the blanks with the superlative forms of the words from the box. You can use some items more than once.

| repairs | cheap | good | economical | extras | expensive |

Victor: Look at these ten cars. Should I get _____the cheapest_____ car?
1.

Simon: _____ is sometimes _____.
2.   3.

Victor: How is that possible?

Simon: The cheapest car sometimes needs _____. You should also consider
                                               4.

fuel economy. Look at this car here. It gets 35 miles per gallon. It's

_____.
5.

Victor: But I like this one _____.
6.

Simon: That one gets only 22 miles per gallon.

Victor: But it has _____: heated seats, a hands-free phone system, a sunroof,
                      7.

and more.

Simon: You want my advice, right? This is my _____ advice.
                                                      8.

WRITING

PART 1 Editing Advice

1. Don't use *-er* and *more* together.

   My new car is ~~more~~ better than my old car.

2. Don't use *-est* and *most* together.

   I want to buy the ~~most~~ cheapest car.

3. Use *than* before the second item of comparison.

   This car is more expensive ^than^ that car.

4. Don't confuse *then* and *than*.

   My English class is easier ~~then~~ *than* my math class.

5. Use *the* before a superlative form.

   Which is ^the^ best college in this city?

6. Don't use *more* in superlative statements.

   My brother is the ~~more~~ *most* interesting person in my family.

7. Use correct spelling with the comparative and superlative forms.

   My brother is the ~~lazyest~~ *laziest* student in his class.

   My English class is ~~biger~~ *bigger* than my art class.

8. Don't use *the* with a possessive form.

   Math is my ~~the~~ worst subject in school.

PART 2 Editing Practice

Some of the shaded words and phrases have mistakes. Find the mistakes and correct them. If the shaded words are correct, write *C*.

Halina wants to get a new job soon. She needs child care for Anna during the day.

Halina: I have to find good child care for Anna. Can you help me find ~~best~~ *the best* one for my family? You
   1.

   know *more* about this *than* I do.
   C
   2.   **3.**

Marta: Let's look for information on the Internet. That's the *easyest* way to get information. Here's a
   4.

   list of ten day care centers in the city.

Halina: Play-Time is *the more expensive*. It's too expensive for me. What about these two, Kiddy-Place
   5.

   and Tiny Tot?

Marta: I think Kiddy Place is more better for you then Tiny-Tot. It's very close to your home. So it's
6.   7.

more convenient for you. How old is Anna now?
8.

Halina: She's two and a half.

Marta: Kiddy-Place only takes children three years old and older. We have to find a place that takes
9.

more younger children.
10.

Halina: What about this one? It's called Baby Bear. It's cheaper Kiddy-Place and closer to my house.
11.   12.

So it's more easy to get to.
13.

Marta: That's a good choice. My sister has three boys, and her the youngest son goes to that child
14.

care. Her son loves it, and she's very happy with it too.

Halina: You always give me best advice. Thanks for your help.
15.

PART 3 Write About It

Look at the photos of the two English classrooms. Use the photos to compare the classes. Write a paragraph of five or six sentences.

Classroom A is...

A

B

PART 4 Learner's Log

1. Write one sentence about each of the topics:
   - Community colleges and four-year universities
   - Comparing used cars

2. Write any questions you still have about community colleges, four-year universities, and comparing used cars.

UNIT

11

Chef Gonzalo Guzman taking a break at a San Francisco restaurant.

CAREERS

Whatever you are, be a good one.
—Abraham Lincoln

1

BEFORE YOU READ

1. What jobs can people get in stores?

2. How do people look for jobs?

READ

Read the following conversation. Pay special attention to the past of the verb *be* in bold.

Halina is talking to Dorota on the phone.

Dorota: Hi, Halina. I stopped by your house several hours ago, but you **weren't** home. Only Anna and Peter **were** there.

Halina: I **was** at BigMart today.

Dorota: **Were** there any good sales?

Halina: I **wasn't** there for the sales. I **was** there to apply for a job as a cashier. Positions are available now for the holidays. A lot of people **were** there, but they **weren't** happy. There **was** a long line to apply for jobs.

Dorota: **Were** there interviews today too?

Halina: No, there **weren't** any interviews. I **was** surprised. The application **was** on a computer at the front of the store. That's where the line was.

Dorota: Many companies have job applications online now. I think you can fill out the application at home.

Halina: I know that now.

Dorota: Employers usually look at the applications and then interview people later if the application is a good one. How **were** the questions on the application? **Were** they hard to answer?

Halina: They **weren't** hard at all. They **were** easy. The first questions **were** about my job history and education. There **were** questions about references too. You **were** one of my references, Dorota. I hope that is okay. They are going to contact you soon.

Dorota: Of course! You can use me as a reference anytime. What **were** some other questions?

Halina: There **were** some tricky questions. One **was**: "Your shift starts at 8:00. Where should you be at 8:00? A) in the parking lot, B) in the employees' room, or C) in your department."

Dorota: That is tricky! What **was** your answer?

Halina: It **wasn't** A or B. Time is important here. It **was** C, of course.

DID YOU KNOW?

For jobs at stores and small businesses there is at least one interview with future employees. For professional jobs, there are often two and sometimes three interviews.

Vocabulary	Context
stop by	I often **stop by** my neighbor's house to visit for a few minutes.
apply for	I want to **apply for** a new job. I have to fill out an application.
position	There are many jobs available at BigMart right now. What **position** do you want to apply for?
the holidays	Store employers often hire extra cashiers in November and December before **the holidays**. It is a busy time of year with Christmas, Hanukkah, and New Year's.
interview (v.) interview (n.)	People from the store are going to talk to me. They are going to **interview** me. The **interview** is tomorrow.
employer/ employee	My **employer** has a big business. He hires new people each year. These people are his **employees**.
as	He uses his past employers **as** references. They work **as** cashiers. She wants a job **as** a manager.
reference	Dorota is a **reference** for Halina. Employers are going to call her. They're going to ask her questions about Halina.
contact	The employer is going to **contact** Mr. Suarez. They are going to call him.
tricky	Some of the questions are **tricky**. They're hard to answer.
shift	My work **shift** starts at 8 a.m. and ends at 5 p.m. The evening **shift** is from 5 p.m. to 1 a.m.

LISTEN

CD 2
TR 36

Listen to the sentences about the conversation. Circle *true* or *false*.

1. (True)   False   5. True   False

2. True   False   6. True   False

3. True   False   7. True   False

4. True   False   8. True   False

11.1 The Past of *Be*—Affirmative Statements

Subject	Be	
I		at the store this morning.
It		crowded.
Dorota		at home.
She	**was**	busy.
Peter		at home.
He		with Anna.
There		a long line at the store.
You		at home.
We		in line.
The questions	**were**	easy.
They		sometimes tricky.
Peter and Anna		in the kitchen.
There		a lot of questions.

EXERCISE 1 Fill in the blanks with *was* or *were*. Use the information from the conversation on page 249.

1. Halina _____*was*_____ at BigMart today.

2. Peter and Anna _____ home.

3. Halina's job application _____ on a computer.

4. Some of the questions _____ tricky.

5. The application _____ easy to fill out.

6. There _____ questions about Halina's job history on the application.

7. People _____ in line for jobs at BigMart today.

8. Dorota _____ at Halina's house today.

9. Positions _____ available today for the holidays.

10. There _____ a question about time.

2

A woman is at a job interview.

BEFORE YOU READ

1. Do you want a job in an office? Why or why not?

2. Where do you want to work? Why?

READ

Read the following conversation. Pay special attention to simple past verbs, affirmative and negative in bold.

Halina: I **had** a job interview today.

Dorota: Great! Was it at BigMart?

Halina: No. I **applied** for a job in an office. I **saw** a job posting online for a sales position a few weeks ago. I **sent** my résumé. And they **called** me yesterday. I **had** the interview this morning.

Dorota: That was fast. How was the interview?

Halina: It **didn't go** well. **I didn't get** there on time. **I didn't find** parking close to the office. I **parked** five blocks away.

Dorota: How late were you?

Halina: Only 15 minutes. I **ran** to the office.

Dorota: That's too late for an interview. Next time, go to the place the day before the interview. You can check travel time and parking then.

Halina: I **didn't like** the interview, Dorota. It **took** an hour. There were two people behind a desk. They **asked** me a lot of questions. And I **felt** nervous.

Dorota: What were some of the questions?

Halina: Well, one question was, "Why do you want this job?" I **told** them the truth. My last job was difficult. I **worked** a lot of hours. I **didn't make** enough money.

Dorota: You shouldn't complain about your past jobs. Instead, say positive things about this new company.

Halina: I **did**. I **told** them some good things. I **said** their company was easy to get to. I **didn't complain** about the parking.

Dorota: But you **didn't say** anything about the company. Find out some information on the company's website. What does the company do? What do you like about it? It's important to know something about the company.

Halina: I **made** a lot of mistakes in this interview. I **said** the wrong things.

Dorota: Don't worry. It was good practice. The next time is going to be easier. You're going to be more prepared.

DID YOU KNOW?
Sometimes companies hire people for 90-day trial periods. If the employee does a good job, he or she can become a regular employee.

🎧 **EXERCISE 7** Complete the conversation between Dorota and Halina about another
CD 2
TR 40 job interview three weeks later. Use the affirmative or negative of the verb given.
Use the simple past.

Halina: Thanks for your advice about interviews, Dorota. Unfortunately,[1]

I _____ *didn't get* _____ the sales position. But I _____ another
　　　　　　1. get　　　　　　　　　　　　　　　　　　　　　**2.** have

interview this morning. It was for a position at another company. I _____
　　　　　　　　　　　　　　　　　　　　　　　　　　　　　　　　　　　3. make

any mistakes this time.

Dorota: That's good.

Halina: I _____ to the building the day before the interview. I
　　　　　　4. drive

_____ a parking lot nearby. I was on time because I
　　5. find

_____ where to park. And I _____ prepared. I
　　6. know　　　　　　　　　　　　　　　　　　　　**7.** be

_____ about the company online first. I _____
　　8. learn　　　　　　　　　　　　　　　　　　　　　　　**9.** tell

the interviewers positive things about their company. I _____ about
　　　　　　　　　　　　　　　　　　　　　　　　　　　　　10. complain

my old job. I was lucky too. They _____ about children. I'm not sure
　　　　　　　　　　　　　　　　　　11. ask

about child care for Anna yet.

Dorota: Don't worry, Halina. They can't ask any personal questions in a job interview.

Halina: Really? Why not?

Dorota: It's against the law.

Halina: I _____ that. I'm glad because personal questions can be tricky.
　　　　　　12. know

―――――――――――
[1] We use *unfortunately* to introduce bad news.

3

GRAMMAR

The Simple Past—
Yes/No Questions

Other Irregular Verbs in the
Simple Past

The Simple Past—
Wh- Questions

The Simple Past—Subject
Questions

More Irregular Verbs in the
Simple Past

CONTEXT

Choosing a Career

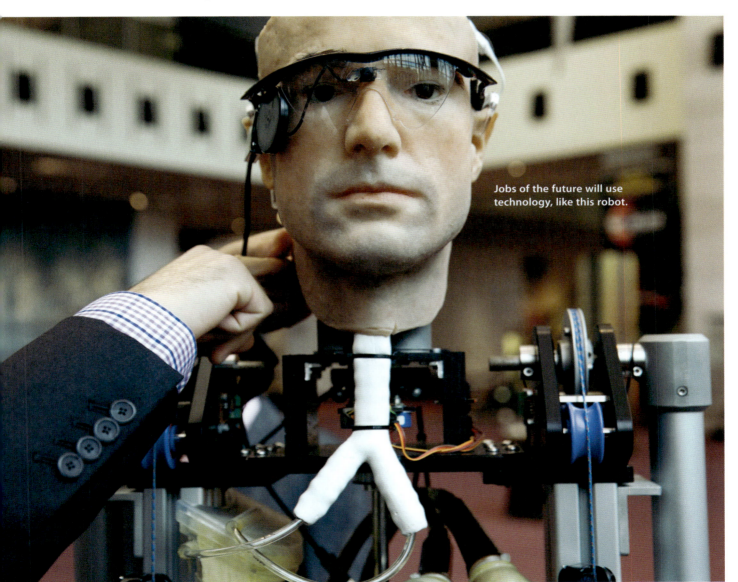

Jobs of the future will use
technology, like this robot.

BEFORE YOU READ

1. Do you know some people with interesting jobs? What kinds of jobs do they have?

2. In your opinion, what jobs are going to be important in the future?

READ

CD 2
TR 41

Read the following conversation. Pay special attention to *yes/no* and *wh-* questions in the simple past in bold.

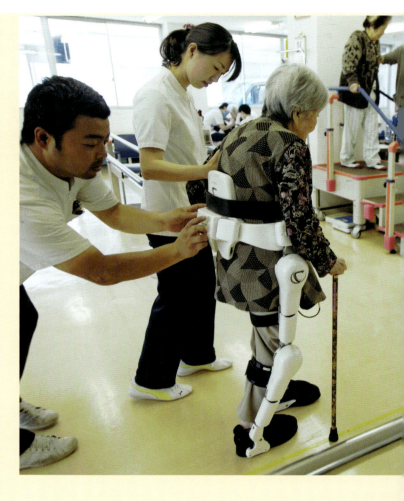

Matt helped Marta's father in the hospital. Simon and Marta became friends with Matt. Now Matt is visiting and they are talking about Matt's job.

Simon: So, Matt, you have an interesting career. You are a physical therapist, right?

Matt: Well, not exactly. I'm a physical therapist assistant, or PTA. I help the physical therapists, or PTs, at the hospital.

Marta: **Why did you choose** this career, Matt?

Matt: Well, I like physical activity. I like to help people. And **did you know** that a job in health services is a good job for the future?

Simon: Yes. I read something about it last week. It's because the U.S. population is getting older.

Matt: That's right. And older people need more health care.

Marta: **What did you do** to prepare for this job?

Matt: First, I took classes at a community college. I was in a special program for physical therapist assistants.

Simon: **How long did it take**?

Matt: Two years. I got a certificate from the college.

Marta: **Did you have** on-the-job training also?

Matt: Yes. We had training at the hospital for 16 weeks. I worked with several physical therapists and their patients. I learned to help people with many different kinds of injuries. I was so busy those days. I had another job too.

Marta: **What did you do**?

Matt: I was a part-time fitness instructor at an athletic club. I thought about a career in fitness.

Simon: **How long did you stay** there?

Matt: Only a year. It was a temporary position.

DID YOU **KNOW?**
Jobs in service industries like health care and hospitality are increasing, while jobs in farming and the postal service are decreasing.

Vocabulary	Context
career	Matt studied for his **career**. He likes his job in health services.
physical therapist (PT)	A **physical therapist** helps patients move and exercise after an accident or injury.
assistant	An **assistant** helps another person with his/her job.
on-the-job training	Companies often give new employees **on-the-job training**. The employees work and learn about the job at the same time.
patient	Marta's father was in the hospital. He was a **patient**.
injure (v.) injury (n.)	She fell and broke her leg. She **injured** her arm too. The **injuries** are very serious.
fitness instructor	A **fitness instructor** works at a health club. He or she helps people with exercise and exercise machines.
athletic club	People go to an **athletic club** to exercise. Sometimes we call an **athletic club** a health club or gym.
temporary	Matt's job was **temporary**. He stayed for only one year.

LISTEN

CD 2
TR 42

Listen to the sentences about the conversation. Circle *true* or *false*.

1. True   (False)   5. True   False

2. True   False   6. True   False

3. True   False   7. True   False

4. True   False   8. True   False

11.11 The Simple Past—*Yes/No* Questions

PART A The question pattern for regular and irregular verbs is the same. We use *did* + the base form.

Did	Subject	Verb (Base Form)		Short Answer
Did	I	**choose**	a good career?	Yes, you did.
Did	Matt	**visit**	Simon and Marta?	Yes, he did.
Did	they	**invite**	Matt to their home?	Yes, they did.
Did	you	**work**	last Saturday?	No, I didn't.
Did	we	**know**	about your last job?	No, you didn't.

Pronunciation Note:

In fast, informal speech, we sometimes pronounce *did you* as /dɪdβə/, and *did he* as /dɪdi/.
Listen to your teacher pronounce the following sentences:

Did you choose a career?   Did he get the job?

Did you make a good choice?   Did he have any training?

continued

PART B Compare the affirmative statements and questions.

Statements	Questions
He **worked** on Saturday.	**Did** he **work** on Sunday?
She **got** the job.	**Did** she **get** a good salary?

EXERCISE 1 Write *yes/no* questions with the words given. Answer them with a short answer. Use the ideas in the conversation on page 268.

1. Matt/need/an education for his job

   Did Matt need an education for his job? Yes, he did.

2. Matt/get/a bachelor's degree

   _____

3. Matt's employer/offer/on-the-job training

   _____

4. Simon and Marta/ask/about Matt's family

   _____

5. Simon/hear/about health careers on TV

   _____

6. Matt/help/Simon's father in the hospital

   _____

7. Simon and Marta/ask/Matt a lot of questions

   _____

8. Matt/work/at the athletic club for many years

   _____

11.12 Other Irregular Verbs in the Simple Past

Base Form	Past Form	Base Form	Past Form	Base Form	Past Form
become	**became**	write	**wrote**	come	**came**
eat	**ate**	spend	**spent**	meet	**met**
choose	**chose**	keep	**kept**	leave	**left**
read	**read**	think	**thought**	hear	**heard**

Pronunciation Note:

The past of *read* sounds like the color *red*.

EXERCISE 2 Fill in the blanks about the conversation on page 268 with the affirmative of a simple past verb. Choose verbs from Chart 11.12 and from Chart 11.9 on page 262. Answers may vary.

1. Matt _____ *spent* _____ two years at a community college.

2. Marta and Simon _____ Matt in the hospital.

3. They all _____ friends.

4. Matt _____ to Simon and Marta's house.

5. Matt _____ a career in health services.

6. Matt _____ about a career as a fitness instructor.

7. Simon _____ about careers in health services last week.

8. It _____ Matt two years to get a certificate from college.

9. Then Matt _____ a full-time job at a hospital.

10. The hospital _____ him on-the-job training.

11. During his training, Matt _____ a temporary job at an athletic club.

12. He _____ his job at the athletic club for only a year. Then he _____ it.
    a.   b.

13. Matt _____ Simon and Marta all about his training.

14. At the hospital, Matt _____ many people with injuries.

15. After his training, Matt _____ how to help people with injuries.

11.13 The Simple Past—*Wh-* Questions

PART A

Question Word(s)	*Did*	Subject	Verb (Base Form)		Answer
Why	**did**	I	**make**	mistakes?	Because you weren't prepared.
What kind of job	**did**	Matt	**find?**		A job as a PTA.
Where	**did**	you	**hear**	about the job?	From a friend.
How	**did**	you	**prepare**	for the job?	I took courses at a community college.
How many people	**did**	they	**interview**	today?	Five.
How long	**did**	they	**work**	at the hospital?	For five years.

PART B Compare affirmative statements and *wh-* questions.

Affirmative Statements	Wh- Questions
Matt **got** his job last year.	How **did** he **get** his job?
Matt **went** to Simon and Marta's house.	Why **did** he **go** to their house?
He **worked** at an athletic club.	When **did** he **work** at an athletic club?

EXERCISE 3 Write a *wh-* question for each answer in the short conversations. The underlined words are the answers. Answers may vary.

1. **A:** How many jobs did he apply for?

   B: He applied for <u>three</u> jobs.

2. **A:** _____

   B: I took classes <u>at Central Community College</u>.

3. **A:** _____

   B: Simon read about <u>careers in health services</u>.

4. **A:** _____

   B: Matt met <u>four</u> physical therapy assistants in that hospital.

5. **A:** _____

   B: They helped <u>people with injuries</u>.

6. **A:** _____

   B: Marta's father stayed in the hospital <u>for three weeks</u>.

7. A: _____

   B: Matt got a part-time job <u>as a fitness instructor</u>.

8. A: _____

   B: He kept that job <u>for a year</u>.

9. A: _____

   B: <u>Because it was a temporary position</u>.

10. A: _____

   B: Simon and Marta met Matt <u>at the hospital</u>.

11.14 The Simple Past—Subject Questions

In a subject question, we use the past form of the verb.

Question Word(s)	Verb -*ed* or Irregular Form		Answer
What	**happened**	to the patient?	She went home.
Who	**helped**	the new patient?	Matt did.
How many students	**got**	a certificate in PT?	Thirty students did.
Which newspaper	**had**	information about health careers?	Last week's newspaper did.

EXERCISE 4 Write questions with the words given. Use the question word as the subject. Use regular and irregular past verbs.

1. Who/take/those people to the hospital

   <u>Who took those people to the hospital?</u>

2. What/happen/at work yesterday

   _____

3. Who/tell/you about that job

   _____

4. How many people/apply/for the job as a fitness instructor

   _____

5. Which patient/spend/two weeks at the hospital

   _____

continued

6. Which student/choose/a job in health services

_____

7. Who/write/about jobs of the future

_____

8. What kinds of patients/need/help with their injuries

_____

9. How many physical therapists/go/to community colleges

_____

10. What/came/in the mail yesterday

_____

11.15 More Irregular Verbs in the Simple Past

Base Form	Past Form	Base Form	Past Form
put	**put**	understand	**understood**
break	**broke**	lose	**lost**
find	**found**	pay	**paid**
drive	**drove**	cost	**cost**
fall	**fell**	buy	**bought**
hurt	**hurt**	sell	**sold**

Language Note:

For some verbs, the base form and the past form are the same. For example, *hurt* and *cost*.

EXERCISE 5 Write a question and an answer for each conversation with the words given.

1. **A:** _Where did the patient hurt her arm?_
   a. Where/the patient/hurt her arm

   B: _She hurt it at the gym._
   b. at the gym

2. **A:** _____
   a. How/she/hurt her arm

   B: _____
   b. fall and break

3. **A:** _____
   a. Which arm/she/break

   B: _____
   b. her right arm

4. **A:** _____
   a. Who/drive/her to the hospital

B: _____
                              b. her husband

5. A: _____
                              a. How long/the woman/stay at the hospital

B: _____
                              b. only a few hours

6. A: _____
                              a. What kind of help/she/get later

B: _____
                              b. physical therapy

7. A: _____
                              a. Who/help/her in her house

B: _____
                              b. a home health care assistant

8. A: _____
                              a. How much/this service/cost

B: _____
                              b. $20 an hour

9. A: _____
                              a. Where/she/find this service

B: _____
                              b. online

10. A: _____
                              a. How much time/she/miss at work

B: _____
                              b. a week

EXERCISE 6 Halina wrote an email to Lisa about her different interviews. Complete the email using the words given. Use contractions when possible.

Hi Lisa,

I just _____*got*_____ your message. I'm so sorry that I _____
          1. get.   **2.** not/call
back. I am so busy! You _____ about my job search. I
                          3. ask
_____ you the details. I _____ an interview three weeks
    4. want/tell   **5.** have
ago for an office job. This morning, I _____ at another company. The first
                                          6. interview
interview _____ well. The second interview _____ much
            7. not/go   **8.** is
better. I _____ confident, and I _____ nervous.
          9. feel   **10.** not/be
    When _____ your job search? _____ your résumé
            11. you/start   **12.** you/send
anywhere yet? Where _____? What about references?
                      13. you/apply
_____ for references? How many references _____?
    14. the company/ask   **15.** you/need/give
_____ you for an interview yet? Which employers _____
    16. the employer/call   **17.** contact
you? Dorota _____ me some great advice: Don't wait to send in your application.
            18. give

    Halina

WRITING

PART 1 Editing Advice

1. Don't use the simple past after *to* (the infinitive).

   spend
   He wanted to ~~spent~~ some time at the athletic club.

2. Use the base form after *did* and *didn't*.

   go
   Where did she ~~went~~ after work?

   find
   They didn't ~~found~~ good jobs.

3. Use the correct verb form and word order in questions.

   did your brother go
   Where ~~your brother went~~ to college?

4. Don't use *did* in subject questions about the past. Use the past form.

   happened
   What ~~did happen~~ at your interview today?

5. Use the correct spelling of the *-ed* forms.

   applied
   She ~~applyed~~ for a job as a fitness instructor.

6. Use the correct verb form. Remember some verbs are irregular.

   hurt   *broke*
   I ~~hurted~~ my leg. He ~~breaked~~ his arm.

PART 2 Editing Practice

Some of the shaded words and phrases have mistakes. Find the mistakes and correct them.
If the shaded words are correct, write *C*.

Matt is talking to a new patient, Teresa, about her injury.

Matt:	Teresa, did your doctor ~~gave~~ *give* you a note for me? 1.
Teresa:	Yes. He gave *C* me this note. 2.
Matt:	Thanks. What happen? How you hurt your shoulder? 3. 4.
Teresa:	I falled during my walk. I broke my shoulder. There was something on the sidewalk and 5. 6. I didn't saw it. 7.
Matt:	That's terrible! Did you called 911? 8.
Teresa:	I wanted to called 911 but I didn't have my cell phone. But someone help me. 9. 10. 11.
Matt:	Who did help you? 12.

Teresa: A nice woman stoped her car to help me.
                                       13.

Matt: What the woman did? Did she took you to the hospital?
               14.   15.

Teresa: No. She call 911 and waited with me. Then the ambulance come and taked me to the
                    16.   17.   18.   19.

hospital. I feeled very nervous. The woman told me not to worry.
            20.   21.

Matt: Did the woman goed with you?
                           22.

Teresa: No, she didn't. I wanted to thanked her later, but she didn't tell me her name.
                                     23.   24.

PART 3 Write About It

Rewrite the following conversation between Matt and Teresa. Change *now* to *last year*. Make the necessary changes to the verbs.

Matt: Do you have a job now, Teresa?

Teresa: Yes, I do. I work in the employment services department at Adams Trucking Company.

Matt: What do you do there?

Teresa: I keep information about employees. I help employees with their problems. And I write

reports. I use the computer a lot.

Matt: How do you get a job like that?

Teresa: Well, it isn't difficult. It takes two years to get a certificate in human resources. Then I have to

send a lot of résumés to different companies.

Matt: Do you like your job?

Teresa: No, I don't. I don't want to work for a company anymore. I'm thinking about a career in

health services like you.

Matt: Did you have a job last year, Teresa?

PART 4 Learner's Log

1. Write one sentence about each topic:
   - Ways to apply for a job
   - Job interviews
   - Training and education for physical therapist assistants.

2. Write any questions you still have about careers in the United States.

VOLUNTEERING

Volunteers help wash a bird after an oil spill, Bursa, California.

Our prime purpose in this life is to help others. And if you can't help them, at least don't hurt them.

— The Dalai Lama

1

GRAMMAR

Review of Verb Tenses—Affirmative and Negative
Review of Infinitives
Review of Modal Verbs—Affirmative and Negative
Review of Time Expressions

CONTEXT

Helping Others

Teaching English in an adult
education center

BEFORE YOU READ

1. What help did you need as a newcomer? Who helped you? How?

2. What do you do to help other newcomers?

READ

CD 2
TR 43

Read the following conversation. Pay special attention to verb tenses and modals in the affirmative and negative.

Simon, Dorota, Victor, Lisa, and Halina are in a coffee shop.

Victor: Simon, thanks for your help on moving day. With your help, it **didn't take** us a long time. You **gave** me some good advice about used cars too. I **don't have** a car yet. I**'m** still **looking**, but I **hope to buy** one soon.

Simon: You're welcome. How**'s** your new apartment? **Are** you adjusted yet?

Lisa: We**'re** very comfortable there. It**'s** big and sunny. Maya **likes** the location because she **didn't have to change** schools. She **doesn't have to walk** far to school. We**'re** all **enjoying** life in the United States now. We **don't feel** like newcomers anymore. Thanks for all your help. We**'re not going to forget** it.

Simon: No problem. Any time.

Halina: And Dorota, I **want to thank** you. With your help, I **learned** about many important places in this city. Also, you **helped** me with my Social Security card. And your advice about job interviews **was** very helpful. I really **like** my new job. I**'m going to stay** with this company for a while.

Dorota: I **was** happy to help, Halina.

Halina: My life **is** easier now. I **don't feel** confused. I **feel** comfortable now. Maybe I **can help** you in your work with newcomers. I **can be** a volunteer. I**'m going to have** some free time on weekends from now on.

Victor: You **can count on** my help too. I **want to volunteer**. Both you and Dorota **were** so helpful when we **arrived**.

Simon: That**'s** good. Marta and I **are going to have** a meeting for volunteers next week. We **have to meet** in the evening. Many people **work** during the day. You **should come**. You **can learn** about other volunteer opportunities too. There **are** many ways to help others.

DID YOU KNOW?

In 2013, 62.8 million Americans volunteered a total of nearly 8 billion hours.

Vocabulary	Context
yet	Victor has a driver's license, but he doesn't have a car **yet**. He will buy a car soon.
comfortable	Halina feels **comfortable** here now. Her life here is easier for her.
newcomer	My friend just arrived in the United States. He is a **newcomer**.
no problem	**No problem** is another way of saying *you're welcome*.
really	Halina **really** likes her new job. She likes it very much.
volunteer (n.) volunteer (v.)	Simon and Dorota are **volunteers**. They **volunteer** with newcomers. They do not get paid for their work.
from now on	Halina has an easier life now. **From now on**, she is going to have more free time.
count on	You always help us. We can always **count on** you.
opportunity	There are many volunteer **opportunities**. You have a choice of many things.

LISTEN

CD 2
TR 44

Listen to the sentences about the conversation. Circle *true* or *false*.

1. True   (False)   6. True   False

2. True   False   7. True   False

3. True   False   8. True   False

4. True   False   9. True   False

5. True   False

12.1 Review of Verb Tenses—Affirmative and Negative

The Simple Present

	Examples	Explanation
Be	a. Dorota **is** forty years old. b. Halina **isn't** a manager now. c. Dorota **is** from Poland. d. The five friends **are** in a coffee shop. e. It **isn't** cold today. f. It **is** 3:00 p.m. g. Halina and Victor **are** happy. Their lives **aren't** as difficult now. h. It **is** hard to start life in a new country.	a. Age b. Occupation/work c. Place of origin d. Location e. Weather f. Time g. Description h. After *it* **in** impersonal expressions
There + Be	a. There **is** a need for volunteers. b. There **aren't** many people in the coffee shop	a. Use *there is* to introduce a singular subject. b. Use *there are* to introduce a plural subject.
Other Verbs	a. Halina **works** in an office. b. Dorota **doesn't work** every day.	a. Facts b. Habits, customs, regular activity

The Present Continuous

Examples	Explanation
Halina **is thanking** Dorota. They **are meeting** in a coffee shop.	Actions at the present moment
Halina **isn't looking** for a job at this time. She **is thinking** about volunteer activities.	Actions at a present time period

The Future

	Examples	Explanation
Be	They **are going to be** volunteers.	
There + Be	There **isn't going to be** a volunteer meeting tomorrow.	Future plans and predictions
Other Verbs	Halina **is going to help** newcomers. Halina **is going to have** more free time soon.	

The Simple Past

	Examples	Explanation
Be	Halina **was** a department manager in Poland.	
There + Be	There **weren't** many people in the coffee shop yesterday.	
Regular Verbs	Victor and Lisa **moved** to a new apartment two weeks ago. They **didn't move** far away.	Actions completed in the past
Irregular Verbs	Halina **got** a job in an office. She **didn't get** a job in a store.	

EXERCISE 1 Complete each sentence about the conversation on page 281 with the correct tense of the verb given. Use affirmative verbs.

1. Halina _____is talking_____ to Dorota now.

　　　　　　talk

2. Simon, Dorota, Halina, Lisa, and Victor _____ together in a coffee shop.

　　　　　　　　　　　　　　　sit

3. Victor's family _____ a bigger apartment.

　　　　　　　find

4. Lisa _____ the new apartment.

　　　　like

5. Victor and Halina _____ life in America now.

　　　　　　　enjoy

6. Simon _____ Victor good advice about used cars.

　　　　　give

7. Victor _____ a used car soon.

　　　　buy

continued

8. Halina and Simon _____ newcomers several months ago.
   be

9. Halina _____ a Social Security card.
   have

10. Dorota _____ Halina with her Social Security card.
    help

11. Halina _____ Dorota with other newcomers from now on.
    help

12. There _____ a volunteer meeting at Marta and Simon's house soon.
    be

EXERCISE 2 Read each sentence. Write sentences using the negative form of the verb and the words given. Use contractions where possible.

1. The five friends are having coffee now.

   <u>They aren't having lunch.</u>
   _____
   lunch

2. Victor and Halina are talking about their lives now.

   _____
   their problems

3. Victor wanted to move.

   _____
   stay in his old apartment

4. His old apartment was too small.

   _____
   big enough for his family

5. Lisa feels comfortable in the United States now.

   _____
   strange anymore

6. Simon gave Victor advice about cars.

   _____
   about jobs

7. Halina and Victor had a lot to do at first.

   _____
   much free time then

8. Victor and Lisa need a used car.

   _____
   a new car

9. Halina's going to work in the same company for a while.

   _____
   look for another job soon

12.2 Review of Infinitives

Examples	Explanation
Halina started **to work** for a new company.	The infinitive is *to* + the base form of the verb.
She expects **to stay** there for a while.	The tense is always in the verb before the infinitive.
I'm happy **to help** you.	Infinitives can go after:
It's fun **to be** a volunteer.	• verbs
It takes time **to learn** about a new country.	• adjectives
Halina wants **to help** other people.	• impersonal expressions with *it*
Victor is trying **to buy** a used car.	

EXERCISE 3 Complete each sentence with an infinitive phrase. Use the ideas from the conversation on page 281 and your own ideas. Answers will vary.

1. It's good _to help other people._

2. Victor wants _____

3. Halina needed _____

4. Halina is planning _____

5. It's not easy _____

6. Simon and Marta like _____

7. Simon and Marta are planning _____

8. Dorota was happy _____

9. I want _____

10. Most immigrants expect _____

11. Students often try _____

12.3 Review of Modal Verbs—Affirmative and Negative

	Examples	Explanation
Can	a. Victor **can speak** Spanish. Dorota **can't speak** Spanish. b. Simon has a license. He **can drive**. Ed **can't drive**. c. Victor and Halina **can volunteer** now. Peter is too busy. He **can't volunteer** now.	a. Ability—no ability b. Permission—no permission c. Possibility—impossibility
Should	a. We **should be** on time. b. You **shouldn't arrive** late to an interview.	a. Advice or suggestion to do something b. Advice not to do something
Must	a. Workers **must have** a Social Security card. b. You **must not drive** without a driver's license.	a. Strong obligation because of a rule or law b. Strong obligation not to do something because of a rule or law
Have To	a. Victor's daughter **has to go** to school. b. She **doesn't have to buy** her lunch at school. She can bring a lunch from home.	a. Necessity (by law, custom, rule, or personal obligation) b. Not necessary

EXERCISE 4 About You Fill in the blanks. Write sentences that are true about you. Use the affirmative or negative of the modals given.

1. I _____*have to*_____ work tonight.
   _{have to}

2. I _____*can't*_____ read the newspaper without a dictionary.
   _{can}

3. I _____ speak English every day.
   _{should}

4. I _____ go to a meeting today.
   _{have to}

5. I _____ speak English like an American yet.
   _{can}

6. I _____ listen to English-language radio to improve my listening skills.
   _{should}

7. I _____ drive.
   _{can}

8. I _____ work.
   _{have to}

EXERCISE 5 Simon, Dorota, Victor, Lisa, and Halina continue their conversation. Fill in the blanks with the correct forms of the verbs given. Use the different tenses, infinitives, and modals.

PART 1:

Dorota: We _____*need*_____ more volunteers this year. There's a lot to do. Sometimes we
   _{1. need}

_____ enough volunteers to help all the newcomers.
   _{2. not/get}

Victor: What else do volunteers do?

Simon: Well, many newcomers _____ how to drive in the United States. They
                                    3. not/know

        _____ sure about the rules on American roads. Volunteers
           4. not/be

        _____ people with their driving practice. Tomorrow, Dorota and I
           5. can/help

        _____ with a group of newcomers. One young man
           6. meet

        _____ to work every day. I _____ with him
           7. have to/drive   **8. practice**

        yesterday. But I _____ busy next week.
                       9. be

Lisa: I _____ him. But we _____ a car yet.
           10. want/help   **11. not/have**

Simon: That's OK. This newcomer _____ a good used car last month. He
                                   12. buy

        _____ someone else's car.
           13. not/need/use

PART 2:

Dorota: Next Thanksgiving, we _____ a holiday dinner for newcomers. We
                                   14. prepare

        _____ volunteers now. It's difficult _____
           15. look for   **16. find**

        people right before a holiday. Everyone is so busy then.

Halina: Peter and I _____ you. I _____.
              17. want/help   **18. can/cook**

Dorota: Thanks, Halina. I _____ my friend Sue about you. Sue and her hus-
                                   19. tell

        band, Rick, _____ holiday meals every year in a school in her
               20. prepare

        neighborhood. Their holiday dinners are very popular with newcomers. Last year, fifty

        newcomers _____. There _____ enough
                       21. come   **22. not/be**

        volunteers. They _____ enough food. So I
                     23. not/have

        _____ them. I _____ the extra food from the
           24. volunteer/help   **25. get**

        deli. Everyone _____ a wonderful time.
                  26. have

12.4 Review of Time Expressions

always	usually	right now	next week	yesterday
never	sometimes	at the moment	soon	last year
from now on	hardly ever	this week	tomorrow	two weeks ago
often	rarely	in a few weeks	right away	every week

EXERCISE 6 Circle the time expressions in the following sentences. Then fill in the blanks in the sentences with an affirmative verb from the box. Use the correct tense. Make contractions where possible. You can use some items more than once. Answers may vary.

help	move	tell	try to get	give	have
be	enjoy	teach	come	find	invite

1. At the coffee shop (yesterday) Dorota _____ told _____ Halina more about her friend Sue.

2. Sue often _____ newcomers.

3. These newcomers hardly ever _____ all the items necessary for their new life in the United States.

4. Sue usually _____ them clothes and things for their house.

5. And she always _____ them about American life.

6. Last year, five new families from Africa _____ into Sue's neighborhood.

7. In just a month, Sue _____ them enough items for a comfortable home.

8. She _____ jobs for them later too.

9. These families _____ their new life in the United States now.

10. Sue _____ all the newcomers to her family's famous holiday dinner later this year.

11. Last year, a city news reporter _____ to Sue's dinner.

12. His report _____ on TV a week later.

13. A lot of people _____ her now.

14. Sue _____ them to work with newcomers now.

EXERCISE 7 Look at the photo. Write a paragraph about the photo. Use all the tenses you learned in this book: simple present, present continuous, future (be *going to*), simple past, and modal verbs. Use affirmative and negative sentences.

_____ *Newcomers are going to have an American Thanksgiving dinner.*

Volunteers cooked a Thanksgiving meal.

_____

_____

_____

_____

_____

_____

_____

_____

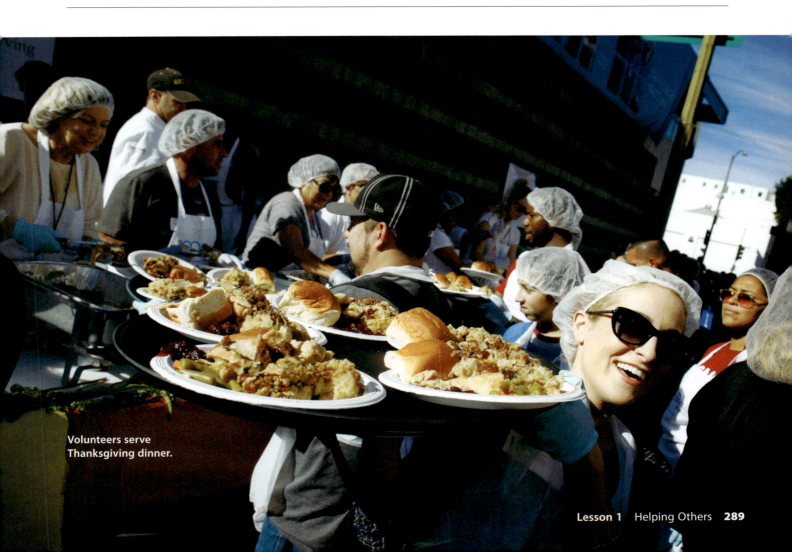

Volunteers serve
Thanksgiving dinner.

2

GRAMMAR
Review of *Yes/No* Questions
Review of *Wh-* Questions

CONTEXT
Volunteer Opportunities

Volunteers build a house in Joplin, Missouri, after a tornado.

BEFORE YOU READ

1. What volunteer opportunities do you know about?

2. Why do people volunteer?

READ

CD 2
TR 46

Read the following conversation. Pay special attention to *yes/no* questions and *wh-* questions in bold.

There's a volunteer meeting at Marta and Simon's house.

Marta: Good evening, everyone. These are my friends Rhonda, Amir, Elsa, and Haru. They're volunteers. They're going to tell you about volunteer work. Rhonda, **are you** ready? **What's your volunteer group doing** this month?

Rhonda: I work for an airline and am a member of a volunteer organization. We have a program to help poor children in other countries. This month we're planning a trip to South America. We're going to bring wheelchairs, eyeglasses, and medical supplies to people in small villages. We will fly there with the supplies.

Marta: **Who gives** you these supplies?

Rhonda: Doctors and hospitals donate medical supplies. Volunteers save their old eyeglasses for us. Charities help us too. And airlines pay for the flights.

Marta: **Do you bring** anything else to these people?

Rhonda: Yes. We bring clothing for children and adults too. And we also have special projects each year.

Marta: **What did your group do** last year, Rhonda? **Was it** another project in South America?

Rhonda: Yes, it was. We brought a sick little boy from Colombia here to the United States. He needed an operation. They didn't have medical care in his village. Two months later, I brought a healthy boy back to his parents. They were so happy. And I was too.

Marta: **Do volunteers have to work** for the airline?

Rhonda: No, there are many ways to volunteer.

Marta: **How can we help**?

Rhonda: You can collect supplies for us.

Marta: **What are you going to do** next?

Rhonda: Right now, we're collecting clothing and toys for a holiday party for Colombian children.

Marta: Rhonda can answer your questions now. **Does anyone have** a question for Rhonda?

DID YOU KNOW?
Most volunteers in the United States are women between the ages of 45 and 54. But volunteers over age 65 give the most hours of their time.

Vocabulary	Context
airline	What **airline** is she going to use to fly to Colombia?
bring	**A:** What did you **bring** to the volunteer meeting? **B:** I **brought** some eyeglasses and clothes.
wheelchair	Some people can't walk. They need a **wheelchair**.
village	Only 500 people live in his **village**.
fly	Rhonda is going to **fly** from New York to Colombia next week.
donate	The wealthy woman is generous. She **donates** a lot of money to charities.
flight	Her **flight** leaves at 5 p.m.
project	Rhonda's **project** is to collect clothing for poor people.
operation	A little boy was very sick. He needed an **operation** at a hospital.
collect	Rhonda **collects** donations to give to poor people.
toy	Children like to play with **toys** such as dolls, cars, and board games.

LISTEN

Listen to the sentences about the conversation. Circle *true* or *false*.

CD 2
TR 47

1. (True)	False	4. True	False	7. True	False
2. True	False	5. True	False	8. True	False
3. True	False	6. True	False	9. True	False

12.5 Review of *Yes/No* Questions

The Simple Present

	Yes/No Questions	Short Answers
Be	**Is** Rhonda a volunteer? **Are** the volunteers from South America?	Yes, she is. No, they aren't.
Be + There	**Is** there a meeting at Marta and Simon's house? **Are** there any Colombians at the meeting?	Yes, there is. No, there aren't.
Other Verbs	**Does** Dorota **work** for an airline? **Do** charities **help** with supplies?	No, she doesn't. Yes, they do.

The Present Continuous

Yes/No Questions	Short Answers
Is Rhonda **talking** about her career?	No, she isn't.
Are you **listening** to Rhonda?	Yes, I am.
Are the volunteers **asking** for money?	No, they aren't.
Are we **learning** about volunteer activities?	Yes, we are.

The Future Tense

Yes/No Questions	Short Answers	
Is Rhonda **going to need** help?	Yes, she is.	
Is there **going to be** a party for the volunteers?	No, there isn't.	
Are new volunteers **going to help**?	Yes, they are.	

The Simple Past

	Yes/No Questions	Short Answers	
Be	**Were** you a volunteer last year? **Was** Rhonda in South America last week? **Were** the volunteers helpful last year?	No, I wasn't. No, she wasn't. Yes, they were.	
Be + There	**Was** there a problem with the volunteers? **Were** there enough volunteers to help?	No, there wasn't. Yes, there were.	
Regular and Irregular Verbs	**Did** Rhonda **help** a sick boy? **Did** volunteers **go** to Mexico?	Yes, she did. No, they didn't.	

Modal Verbs and *Have To*

	Yes/No Questions	Short Answers	
Should	**Should** we volunteer for that project?	Yes, we should.	
Can	**Can** I volunteer?	Yes, you can.	
Have To	**Did** Rhonda **have to** volunteer for this project? **Do** volunteers **have to** come to the meeting?	No, she didn't. Yes, they do.	

Language Note:

Questions with *must* are not common. We use *have to* for questions.

EXERCISE 1 Write *a yes/no* question about the conversation on page 291. Use the words given. Use the same tense as in the statement. Answer your question with a short answer.

1. Rhonda has a job.

   <u>Does she have a job with an airline? Yes, she does.</u>
   with an airline

2. Rhonda is talking.

   _____
   about her job with the airline

3. Rhonda brings medical supplies to poor children.

   _____
   wheelchairs

4. A little boy needed medical care last year.

   _____
   an operation

   continued

5. The sick boy was from a village.

_____
from the United States

6. Rhonda brought the boy to the United States.

_____
back to his parents

7. The volunteers are going to have a party.

_____
in the United States

8. There are many people at Marta and Simon's house today.

_____
any volunteers

9. People should save their medical supplies for Rhonda's projects.

_____
toys too

10. People can ask Rhonda questions.

_____
about other projects

12.6 Review of *Wh-* Questions

The Simple Present

	Wh- Questions	**Answers**
Be	Who **is** Rhonda? Where **are** the volunteers?	She's Marta's friend. They're at Marta and Simon's house.
Be + There	Why **is** there a meeting today? How many people **are** there at the meeting?	To give information about volunteer work. About twenty.
Subject Questions	Who **collects** eyeglasses? Which airline **helps** people?	Many people do. Rhonda's airline does.
Other Questions	Where **does** Rhonda **work**? How **do** doctors **help**?	At an airline. They give medical supplies.

The Present Continuous

	Wh- Questions	**Answers**
Subject Questions	How many volunteers **are speaking** at the meeting?	Three.
Other Questions	What kind of trip **is** Rhonda **planning**? What **are** volunteers **collecting** now?	A trip to bring supplies to South America. Children's clothing and toys

The Future with *Be Going To*

	Wh- Questions	Answers
Be	What **is** the new project **going to be**? When **are** you **going to be** a volunteer?	A holiday party for kids. Next month.
Be + There	When **is** there **going to be** another meeting? How many meetings **are** there **going to be**?	Next week. Only two more.
Subject Questions	Which children **are going to get** the gifts? Who **is going to be** at the next meeting?	The children in one small village. Many new volunteers.
Other Questions	What **is** Rhonda **going to do** with the toys? When **are** the volunteers **going to give** the toys to the children?	She's going to give them to kids. In December.

The Simple Past

	Wh- Questions	Answers
Be	Where **was** the last meeting? Why **were** the sick boy's parents worried?	We don't know. Because there was no medical care in their village.
Be + There	Why **were** there people at their house? What kind of help **was** there for the boy?	Because there was a meeting about volunteer work. Medical help.
Subject Questions	Which volunteers **brought** the boy to the U.S.? Who **came** to the meeting?	Rhonda and her friends did. Victor and Lisa did.
Other Questions	What **did** the boy **need**? When **did** the boy **have** his operation?	He needed an operation. He had it last year.

Modal Verbs and *Have To*

	Wh- Questions	Answers
Subject Questions	Who **can** help Rhonda? How many children **had to** get an operation last year?	All of us can help her. One did.
Other Questions	When **can** we help Rhonda? What **should** we bring to Rhonda? When **does** Rhonda **have to** get the toys?	You can help right now. You should bring her clothing and toys. Before her next trip.

Language Note:

Questions with *must* are not common. Use *have to* for questions.

EXERCISE 2 Write a *wh-* question about each sentence. Use the question words given. Then write the answers. Use the ideas in the conversation on page 291.

1. Rhonda has a job.

   <u>What kind of job does she have? She works for an airline.</u>
   what kind

2. Rhonda does volunteer work.

   _____
   what kind

3. Rhonda went to South America last year.

   _____
   why

4. Someone pays for the flights to South America.

   _____
   who

5. The volunteers are going to have a party for children.

   _____
   when

6. A sick boy had to come to the United States.

   _____
   why

7. People can help with the holiday project.

   _____
   how

8. We should collect things for Rhonda.

   _____
   what

9. Rhonda is explaining something to the new volunteers.

   _____
   what

EXERCISE 3 Look at the photo of a food bank on page 297. Write *yes/no* questions and *wh-* questions about the photo. Use a different tense in each question: simple present, present continuous, future, and past. You can use modal verbs too. Write the answers.

1. <u>Are there people at the food bank? Yes, there are.</u>

2. _____

3. _____

4. _____

5. _____

EXERCISE 4 Amir, another volunteer, is talking now. People are asking him questions. Complete each question with the words given. Use the answer to help you choose the tense.

Victor: Where _____ *do you volunteer* _____ ?
1. you/volunteer

Amir: I volunteer in my neighborhood. I work at a child-care center once a week for low-income families. There are other volunteers too. We help with the children. We also plan projects for them.

Halina: How many _____ at the center?
2. children/there

Amir: Every day is different. There are usually about 15 or 20 kids.

Simon: How many hours _____ ?
3. each volunteer/have to/work

Amir: Usually four to six hours. But sometimes we work more. Last week was one of those weeks.

Victor: What _____ last week?
4. happen

Amir: We had 10 new kids, so I worked an extra day to help.

Halina: What _____ ?
5. you/do

Amir: I helped with the art activities, I served the meals, and I played with the children a lot.

Simon: How _____ about this day care center?
6. you/learn

Amir: It was on our city's website. That's a good place to look for volunteer opportunities.

Marta: What project _____ now?
7. the volunteers/plan

Amir: We're planning a talent show and sale of the children's art. We're going to charge admission.

Victor: What _____ for the show?
8. children/learn/do

Amir: They're learning to sing several songs and they also dance.

Simon: When _____ ?
9. the show/be

Amir: In three months. I can tell you the date later.

Halina: What _____ with the money?
10. center/do

Amir: We are going to buy books for the children's library. We are also going to buy new art supplies.

EXERCISE 5 Elsa, another volunteer, is talking now. People are asking Elsa questions. Complete each question with the words given. Use the answers to help you choose the tense.

Marta: This is Elsa. She volunteers to help older people. She works with a neighborhood group. She works one week each month.

Woman: _____ Are you going to work _____ this week, Elsa?
                                    1. you/work

Elsa: Yes, I am. I'm going to help an older woman in my neighborhood. She can't see very well and she lives alone.

Man: How _____ her?
                        2. you/help

Elsa: I'm going to take her to a doctor's appointment tomorrow, and I'm going to take her to the supermarket on the weekend.

Woman: What _____ all day?
                            3. this woman/do

Elsa: She goes to the gym two days a week. She exercises in a swimming pool.

Woman: _____ the bus to the gym?
                    4. she/have to/take

Elsa: No, she doesn't. Another volunteer takes her.

Woman: _____ ?
                        5. she/can/swim

Elsa: She doesn't exactly swim. She takes an exercise class for seniors. It's exercise in the water.

Woman: When _____ these classes?
                            6. she/start

Elsa: She started the classes twenty years ago. She says, "This class is responsible for my long life."

She's ninety years old!

Man: How _____ this job, Elsa?
  7. find

Elsa: I heard about it from a friend in the neighborhood. We're always looking for more volunteers.

Who _____ us?
  8. want/help

Woman: I do! When _____ ?
  9. I/can/start

EXERCISE 6 Read the FAQs (Frequently Asked Questions) from a volunteer organization's website. Complete the sentences with the correct form of the words given.

1. What _____ *does our organization do* _____ ?
     a. our organization/do

   We are an umbrella organization, which means we _____ with a lot of
                                                      b. work

   smaller groups. We _____ volunteers with opportunities.
                         c. help/match

2. How _____ ?
      a. volunteers/help

   Our volunteers _____ all kinds of things: build houses, translate at
                     b. do

   hospitals, clean up parks, and serve food at the homeless shelter. If someone

   _____ something special, we
        c. can/do

   _____ a place for him or her.
        d. try/find

3. When _____ ?
       a. you/need/volunteers

   Our community _____ volunteers all the time. Last year, more than
                     b. need

   8,000 volunteers _____ about 40,000 hours to different projects. We
                        c. give

   think we _____ even more volunteers in the next 12 months. Many
               d. have

   people _____ around the holidays, but we actually
             e. want/volunteer

   _____ volunteers year-round.
        f. use

4. What _____ to get started?
       a. I/should/do

   You _____ an application online. Please
          b. should/fill out

   _____ us a lot about yourself so we
        c. tell

   _____ you with the right job. In a week or so, someone
        d. can/match

   _____ you to schedule an interview.
        e. call

WRITING

PART 1 Editing Advice

1. Use the base form after *doesn't, don't, didn't, have to*, and modals.

   Peter didn't ~~went~~ *go* to the meeting last Saturday.

   He had to ~~worked~~ *work* last Saturday.

   Volunteers should ~~to go~~ *go* to the meetings.

2. Don't forget to use the base form in an infinitive.

   They wanted to ~~helped~~ *help* us with the project.

3. Don't use a form of *be* with the simple present or simple past.

   Elsa's neighbor ~~is go~~ *goes* to the store every week.

   She ~~was walk~~ *walked* to the store yesterday.

4. Don't use statement word order in a question.

   Where ~~he worked~~ *did he work* last year?

   When ~~Elsa is going to drive~~ *is Elsa going to drive* her neighbor to the supermarket?

5. Don't use *do, does*, or *did* in a subject question.

   Who ~~does work~~ *works* as a volunteer?

6. Be sure each verb is in the correct tense and form for the context.

   Everyone ~~leaves~~ *left* the meeting at 10 o'clock last night.

   The older woman ~~is going~~ *goes* to the gym two days a week.

7. Use the correct form in a short answer.

   Are you a volunteer? No, ~~I don't~~ *I'm not*.

PART 2 Editing Practice

Some of the shaded words and phrases have mistakes. Find the mistakes and correct them.
If the shaded words are correct, write *C*.

Marta is interviewing another volunteer, Haru, at the meeting.

Marta: What kind of volunteer job ∧ you have? *do*
                                          1.

Haru: I work at a nature museum. I teach children's groups about animals, birds, and plants. Last   *C*
           2.

           month some students come to do a school project. I was helped them. They had to wrote a
                              3.   **4.**   **5.**

           report about the birds in our museum. They didn't knew about these birds before.
                                                          6.

Marta: That's interesting. Where did you heard about this job?
                                      7.

300   Unit 12

Haru: I finded it through *United We Serve*. It's a way for us to volunteer in our own communities.
8.

There's a great website for volunteers. Go to www.serve.gov.
9.

Marta: How this site works?
10.

Haru: You fill in your interests and your location: your zip code or city and state. Then, the website

list many opportunities. It's easy use. You doesn't have to look at many different sites.
11.   12.   13.

Marta: It's just for young people?
14.

Haru: No, it doesn't. There are opportunities for everyone! Older people can click on the link for
15.

Senior Corps for information.

Marta: I'm have an idea for a volunteer project. What should I do?
16.   17.

Haru: The website has *toolkits*. A *toolkit* is a list of steps to follow. Before you start, you should to put
18.

your idea on the site and ask for volunteers. Many people are volunteering these days. And
19.

more people going to volunteer in the future. In October 2009, the government pass a law called
20.   21.

the Serve America Act. Now student volunteers can get money for their education. And the

number of older people is going up. That means we going to have more older volunteers too.
22.   23.

Marta: Thank you for your time Haru. You're going to stay for coffee with us?
24.

Haru: Yes, I do. Thank you. But I have to leave by 8:30.
25.   26.

PART 3 Write About It

Answer one of the following questions. Write a paragraph and use affirmative and negative statements in the correct tense.

- Do you know a volunteer in the United States? What does this volunteer do?
- Do you want to be a volunteer? What are you going to do? Why?
- Were you (or was someone you know) a volunteer in your country? Write about the volunteer activity.
- Did a volunteer help you? How?

    My neighbor Javier is a volunteer. He collects donations for the local food bank...

PART 4 Learner's Log

1. Write one sentence about each of the volunteers from this unit. Use a different tense in each sentence.
2. Write any questions you still have about volunteer work.

Vowel and Consonant Pronunciation Charts

Vowels

Symbol	Examples
ʌ	love, cup
a	father, box
æ	class, black
ə	alone, atom
ɛ	ever, well
i	eat, feet
ɪ	miss, bit
ɔ	talk, corn
ʊ	would, book
oʊ	cone, boat
u	tooth, through
eɪ	able, day
aɪ	mine, try
aʊ	about, cow
ɔɪ	join, boy

Consonants

Symbol	Examples
b	bread, cab
d	door, dude
f	form, if
g	go, flag
h	hello, behind
j	use, yellow
k	cook, hike
l	leg, little
m	month, time
n	never, nine
ŋ	singer, walking
p	put, map
r	river, try
s	saw, parks
ʃ	show, action
ɾ	atom, lady
t	take, tent
tʃ	check, church
θ	thing, both
ð	the, either
v	voice, of
w	would, reward
z	zoo, mazes
ʒ	usual, vision
dʒ	just, edge

The Calendar

Months	Days	Seasons
January (Jan.)	Sunday (Sun.)	Winter
February (Feb.)	Monday (Mon.)	Spring
March (Mar.)	Tuesday (Tues.)	Summer
April (Apr.)	Wednesday (Wed.)	Fall or Autumn
May	Thursday (Thurs.)	
June (Jun.)	Friday (Fri.)	
July (Jul.)	Saturday (Sat.)	
August (Aug.)		
September (Sept.)		
October (Oct.)		
November (Nov.)		
December (Dec.)		

Dates

January 6, 1999
Jan. 6, 1999
1/6/1999
1/6/99
1-6-99

March 27, 2017
Mar. 27, 2017
3/27/2017
3/27/17
3-27-17

continued

Numbers

Cardinal Numbers	Ordinal Numbers
1 = one	first
2 = two	second
3 = three	third
4 = four	fourth
5 = five	fifth
6 = six	sixth
7 = seven	seventh
8 = eight	eighth
9 = nine	ninth
10 = ten	tenth
11 = eleven	eleventh
12 = twelve	twelfth
13 = thirteen	thirteenth
14 = fourteen	fourteenth
15 = fifteen	fifteenth
16 = sixteen	sixteenth
17 = seventeen	seventeenth
18 = eighteen	eighteenth
19 = nineteen	nineteenth
20 = twenty	twentieth
21 = twenty-one	twenty-first
30 = thirty	thirtieth
40 = forty	fortieth
50 = fifty	fiftieth
60 = sixty	sixtieth
70 = seventy	seventieth
80 = eighty	eightieth
90 = ninety	ninetieth
100 = one hundred	hundredth
1,000 = one thousand	thousandth
1,000,000 = one million	millionth

Peter Thomas
17 Cherry Tree Lane
New York, NY 10001

6-38/542   7024

DATE September 6, 2010

PAY TO THE
ORDER OF _Teresa Jones_ $ 950 00/100

Nine Hundred Fifty and 00/100 ————— DOLLARS

Summerville Bank

FOR _rent_   _Peter Thomas_

⑆0123456789⑆ 0123456789101⑈ 7024

Spelling Rules for Verbs and Nouns

Spelling of the -s Form of Verbs and Nouns

Verbs	Nouns	Rule
visit—visits need—needs like—likes spend—spends see—sees	chair—chairs bed—beds truck—trucks gift—gifts bee—bees	Add -s to most words to make the -s form.
mi<u>ss</u>—misses wa<u>sh</u>—washes cat<u>ch</u>—catches fi<u>x</u>—fixes	dre<u>ss</u>—dresses di<u>sh</u>—dishes mat<u>ch</u>—matches bo<u>x</u>—boxes	Add -es to base forms with ss, sh, ch, and x at the end.
worr<u>y</u>—worries tr<u>y</u>—tries stud<u>y</u>—studies	part<u>y</u>—parties cit<u>y</u>—cities berr<u>y</u>—berries	If the word ends in a consonant + y, change y to i and add -es.
pa<u>y</u>—pays pla<u>y</u>—plays enjo<u>y</u>—enjoys	bo<u>y</u>—boys da<u>y</u>—days ke<u>y</u>—keys	If the word ends in a vowel + y, do not change the y. Just add -s.
	lea<u>f</u>—leaves kni<u>fe</u>—knives	If the noun ends in f or fe, change f or fe to ves.

Irregular -s Forms of Verbs
have—has go—goes do—does

Irregular Plural Forms of Nouns	
man—men woman—women child—children mouse—mice	foot—feet tooth—teeth person—people (or persons) fish—fish

continued

Spelling of the *-ing* Forms of Verbs

Verbs	Rule
go—go**ing** eat—eat**ing** spend—spend**ing**	Add *-ing* to most verbs to make the *-ing* form.
tak<u>e</u>—tak**ing** writ<u>e</u>—writ**ing** mak<u>e</u>—mak**ing**	If a verb ends in silent *e*, drop the *e* and add *-ing*. Do NOT double the final consonant. Wrong: writting
pay—pay**ing** buy—buy**ing** worry—worry**ing** study—study**ing**	If a verb ends in a *y*, just add *-ing*. Wrong: studing
sto<u>p</u>—sto**pping** ru<u>n</u>—ru**nning** spl<u>it</u>—spli**tting**	If a one-syllable verb ends in consonant + vowel + consonant, double the final consonant and add *-ing*.
begín—begi**nning** permít—permi**tting** occúr—occu**rring**	If a two–syllable word ends in consonant + vowel + consonant, double the final consonant and add *-ing* only if the last syllable is stressed.
ópen—open**ing** háppen—happen**ing** devélop—develop**ing**	If a multi-syllable word ends in consonant + vowel + consonant and the final syllable is not stressed, do NOT double the final consonant. Just add *-ing*.

Spelling of the *-ed* Forms of Regular Past Tense Verbs

Verbs	Rule
listen—listen**ed** look—look**ed**	Add *-ed* to most regular verbs to form the past tense.
bak<u>e</u>—bake**d** smil<u>e</u>—smile**d** sav<u>e</u>—save**d**	If a verb ends in silent *e*, just add *-d*.
worr<u>y</u>—worr**ied** stud<u>y</u>—stud**ied**	If a verb ends in a consonant + *y*, change the *y* to *i* and add *-ed*.
enjoy—enjoy**ed** delay—delay**ed**	If a verb ends in a vowel + *y*, just add *-ed*.
sto<u>p</u>—sto**pped** dra<u>g</u>—dra**gged** sla<u>m</u>—sla**mmed**	If a one-syllable verb ends in consonant + vowel + consonant, double the final consonant and add *-ed*.
permít—permi**tted** occúr—occu**rred**	If a two–syllable verb ends in consonant + vowel + consonant, double the final consonant and add *-ed* only if the last syllable is stressed.
ópen—open**ed** háppen—happen**ed** devélop—develop**ed**	If a multi-syllable verb ends in consonant + vowel + consonant and the final syllable is not stressed, do NOT double the final consonant. Just add *-ed*.

Spelling Rules for Comparative and Superlative Forms

Simple Form	Comparative Form	Superlative Form	Rule
old cheap	old**er** cheap**er**	old**est** cheap**est**	Add -er and -est to most adjectives.
big hot	big**ger** hot**ter**	big**gest** hot**test**	If the adjective ends with consonant + vowel + consonant, double the final consonant before adding -er or -est.
nice late	nice**r** late**r**	nice**st** late**st**	If the adjective ends in e, add -r or -st only.
busy easy	bus**ier** eas**ier**	bus**iest** eas**iest**	If the adjective ends in y, change y to i and add -er or -est.

Alphabetical List of Irregular Past Forms

Base Form	Past Form	Base Form	Past Form
be	was/were	lend	lent
become	became	let	let
begin	began	lie[1]	lay
bend	bent	light	lit (or lighted)
bet	bet	lose	lost
bite	bit	make	made
blow	blew	mean	meant
break	broke	meet	met
bring	brought	mistake	mistook
build	built	pay	paid
buy	bought	put	put
catch	caught	quit	quit
choose	chose	read	read[2]
come	came	ride	rode
cost	cost	ring	rang
cut	cut	run	ran
do	did	say	said
draw	drew	see	saw
drink	drank	sell	sold
drive	drove	send	sent
eat	ate	shake	shook
fall	fell	shoot	shot
feed	fed	shut	shut
feel	felt	sing	sang
fight	fought	sit	sat
find	found	sleep	slept
fit	fit	speak	spoke
fly	flew	spend	spent
forget	forgot	spread	spread
get	got	stand	stood
give	gave	steal	stole
go	went	swim	swam
grow	grew	take	took
have	had	teach	taught
hear	heard	tear	tore
hide	hid	tell	told
hit	hit	think	thought
hold	held	throw	threw
hurt	hurt	understand	understood
keep	kept	wake	woke
know	knew	wear	wore
lead	led	win	won
leave	left	write	wrote

[1] When *lie* means to not tell the truth, the past form is *lied*. When it means to place something down, the past form is *lay*.

[2] We pronounce the past tense of *read* like the color *red*.

Capitalization Rules

Rule	Example
The first word in a sentence	**M**y friends are helpful.
The word "I"	My sister and **I** took a trip together.
Names of people	**A**braham **L**incoln; **G**eorge **W**ashington
Titles preceding names of people	**D**octor (**D**r.) **S**mith; **P**resident **L**incoln; **Q**ueen **E**lizabeth; **M**r. **R**ogers; **M**rs. **C**arter
Geographic names	the **U**nited **S**tates; **L**ake **S**uperior; **C**alifornia; the **R**ocky **M**ountains; the **M**ississippi **R**iver NOTE: The word "the" in a geographic name is not capitalized.
Street names	**P**ennsylvania **A**venue (**A**ve.); **W**all **S**treet (**S**t.); **A**bbey **R**oad (**R**d.)
Names of organizations, companies, colleges, buildings, stores, hotels	the **R**epublican **P**arty; **C**engage **L**earning; **D**artmouth **C**ollege; the **U**niversity of **W**isconsin; the **W**hite **H**ouse; **B**loomingdale's; the **H**ilton **H**otel
Nationalities and ethnic groups	**M**exicans; **C**anadians; **S**paniards; **A**mericans; **J**ews; **K**urds; **I**nuit
Languages	**E**nglish; **S**panish; **P**olish; **V**ietnamese; **R**ussian
Months	**J**anuary; **F**ebruary
Days	**S**unday; **M**onday
Holidays	**I**ndependence **D**ay; **T**hanksgiving
Important words in a title	*Grammar in Context; The Old Man and the Sea; Romeo and Juliet; The Sound of Music* NOTE: Capitalize "the" as the first word of a title.

Map of the United States of America

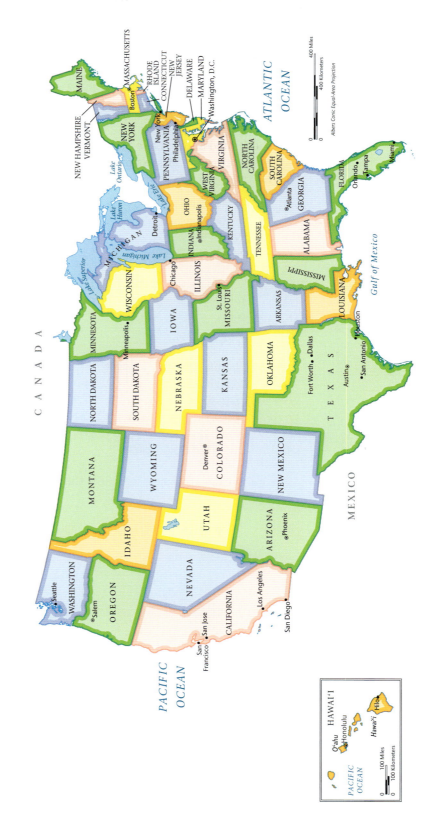

U.S. State Abbreviations

AL	Alabama	MT	Montana
AK	Alaska	NE	Nebraska
AZ	Arizona	NV	Nevada
AR	Arkansas	NH	New Hampshire
CA	California	NJ	New Jersey
CO	Colorado	NM	New Mexico
CT	Connecticut	NY	New York
DE	Delaware	NC	North Carolina
FL	Florida	ND	North Dakota
GA	Georgia	OH	Ohio
HI	Hawaii	OK	Oklahoma
ID	Idaho	OR	Oregon
IL	Illinois	PA	Pennsylvania
IN	Indiana	RI	Rhode Island
IA	Iowa	SC	South Carolina
KS	Kansas	SD	South Dakota
KY	Kentucky	TN	Tennessee
LA	Louisiana	TX	Texas
ME	Maine	UT	Utah
MD	Maryland	VT	Vermont
MA	Massachusetts	VA	Virginia
MI	Michigan	WA	Washington
MN	Minnesota	WV	West Virginia
MS	Mississippi	WI	Wisconsin
MO	Missouri	WY	Wyoming
		DC*	District of Columbia

*The District of Columbia is not a state. Washington, D.C., is the capital of the United States.

Note: Washington, D.C., and Washington state are not the same.

Vocabulary in Context Index

Vocabulary Word(s)	Page Number	Vocabulary Word(s)	Page Number
deliver	82	get (to a place)	260
depend on	236	gift	200
deposit	188	go shopping	149
desk job	88	grain	123
difference between	166	guideline	123
different	5	gym	88
difficult	260	hard	17
dirty	11	hardware store	157
do errands	178	have fun	65
don't worry	11	headache	149
downstairs	157	help/helpful	5
drive-through	188	high chair	199
during	88	hire	210
each other	65	hold/hold hands	178
early	17	holiday/holidays	29, 250
economical	236	home supply store	157
education	225	hungry	82
elevator	157	hurt	110
employer/employee	250	identity document	51
empty	11	immigrant	5
enjoy	65	in a hurry	100
enough	157	income/low-income	123
enter	56	infant	110
everything	5	information	51
excited	200	injure	269
exercise	88	injury	269
expect	73	inside	34
expensive	56	instead	260
extra	73	interview	250
extras	236	invite/invitation	65
fast	29	item	9
fat	123	job	73
favorite	129	keep	73
fill out	51	kid	29
financial aid	56	lamp	157
fitness instructor	269	laundromat	5
fly/flight	292	law	100
for a while	199	learner's permit	100
forget	51	less than	123
free	17	let	51
free time	65	life	5
from now on	282	like	236
fuel economy	236	lightbulb	157
full-time	73	line	178
furniture	199	look up	56
get paid	73	lunch box	129
get some sleep	200	mailing supplies	178

Vocabulary Word(s)	Page Number	Vocabulary Word(s)	Page Number
make a decision	236	PIN	40
make a mistake	260	polite	33
make money	73	popular	65
maybe	188	position	250
meal	82	positive	260
mean	73	postage	178
mechanic	236	pound	17
messenger	88	practice	100
microphone	189	prefer	157
middle initial	56	prepared	260
mileage	236	prepared food	82
move/mover	210	price	17
necessary	11	print	51, 178
neighborhood	210	probably	188
nervous	260	product	17
never	33	program	149
newcomer	282	project	292
news	149	public school	137
note	137	pump	110
nutrition	123	really	282
offer	225	reference	250
on (my, your, etc.) mind	33	relative	200
on sale	17	relax	73
on the way	110	rent	210
on time	29	repair	236
online	56	resale shop	199
on-the-job training	269	résumé	260
operation	292	return	137
opportunity	282	ride a bicycle/bike	88
order	82	right	8
ounce	166	roll	189
out of	40	rule	100
outdoor concert	65	safety	100
outlet mall	110	salary	73
outside	33	sales position	260
over	100	same	17
overtime	73	sample	17
pack	210	save	100
package	17, 178	scale	178
park	87	school supplies	137
part-time	73	seat belt	110
pass a test	100	secret	40
passenger	110	security guard	40
patient	269	self checkout	17
pharmacy	149	self-service	178
physical therapist (PT)	269	serious	33
pick up	178	serve	123

- **Adjective** An adjective gives a description of a noun.

    It's a *tall* tree. He's an *old* man. My sisters are *nice*.

- **Adverb** An adverb describes the action of a sentence or an adjective or another adverb.

    She speaks English *fluently*. I drive *carefully*.

    She speaks English *extremely well*. She is *very* intelligent.

- **Affirmative** means "yes."

- **Apostrophe '** We use the apostrophe for possession and contractions.

    My *sister's* friend is beautiful. (possession) Today *isn't* Sunday. (contraction)

- **Article** An article comes before a noun. It tells if the noun is definite or indefinite. The definite article is *the*. The indefinite articles are *a* and *an*.

    I have *a* cat. I ate *an* apple. *The* teacher is helpful.

- **Base Form** The base form, sometimes called the "simple" form, of the verb has no tense. It has no ending (-*s* or -*ed*): *be, go, eat, take, write*.

    I didn't *go* out. He doesn't *know* the answer.

    You shouldn't *talk* in the library.

- **Capital Letter** A B C D E F G . . .

- **Comma** ,

- **Comparative Form** A comparative form of an adjective or adverb is used to compare two things.

    My house is *bigger* than your house.

    Her husband drives *faster* than she does.

- **Complement** The complement of the sentence is the information after the verb if it is not an object. It completes the verb phrase.

    He works *hard*. I slept *for five hours*. They are *late*.

- **Consonant** The following letters are consonants: *b, c, d, f, g, h, j, k, l, m, n, p, q, r, s, t, v, w, x, y, z*.

    Note: *y* is sometimes considered a vowel, as in the word *syllable*.

- **Contraction** A contraction is two words joined with an apostrophe.

    He's my brother. *You're* late. *What's* your name?

    (*He's = He is*) (*You're = You are*) (*What's = What is*)

- **Count Noun** Count nouns are nouns that we can count. They have a singular and a plural form.

    1 pen — 3 pens 1 table — 4 tables

- **Frequency Words** Frequency words (*always, usually, often, sometimes, rarely, seldom, hardly ever*, and *never*) tell how often an action happens.

    I *never* drink coffee. We *always* do our homework.

- **Imperative** An imperative sentence gives a command or instructions. An imperative sentence omits the subject pronoun *you*.

    Come here.   *Don't be* late.   Please *sit* down.

- **Infinitive** An infinitive is *to* + the base form.

    I want *to leave*.   You need *to be* here on time.

- **Modal** The modal verbs are *can, could, shall, should, will, would, may, might,* and *must*.

    They *should* leave.   I *must* go.

- **Negative** means "no."

- **Nonaction Verb** A nonaction verb has no action. We do not usually use a continuous tense (*be* + verb *–ing*) with a nonaction verb. The nonaction verbs are: *believe, cost, care, have, hear, know, like, love, matter, mean, need, own, prefer, remember, see, seem, think, understand, want,* and sense-perception verbs.

    She *has* a computer.   We *love* our mother.   You *look* tired.

- **Noncount Noun** A noncount noun is a noun that we don't count. It has no plural form.

    She drank some *water*.   He ate some *rice*.

    I need *money*.   We had a lot of *homework*.

- **Noun** A noun is a person (*brother*), a place (*kitchen*), or a thing (*table*). Nouns can be either count (*1 table, 2 tables*) or noncount (*money, water*).

    My *brother* lives in California.   My *sisters* live in New York.

    I get *money* from my parents.   Everyone needs *love*.

- **Object** The object of the sentence follows the verb. It receives the action of the verb.

    He bought *a car*.   I saw *a movie*.   I met *your brother*.

- **Object Pronoun** Use object pronouns (*me, you, him, her, it, us,* and *them*) after the verb or preposition.

    He likes *her*.   I saw the movie. Let's talk about *it*.

- **Parentheses** ( )

- **Period** .

- **Phrase** A group of words that go together.

    Last month my sister came to visit.   There is a red car *in front of my house*.

- **Plural** means "more than one." A plural noun usually ends with *-s* or *-es*.

    She has beautiful *eyes*.   Please wash the *dishes*.

- **Possessive Form** Possessive forms show ownership or relationship.

    Mary's coat is in the closet.   *My* brother lives in Miami.

- **Preposition** A preposition is a connecting word: *about, above, across, after, around, as, at, away, before, behind, below, by, down, for, from, in, into, like, of, off, on, out, over, to, under, up,* and *with*.

    The book is *on* the table.   I live *with* my parents.

- **Present Participle** The present participle is verb + –*ing*.

  She is *sleeping*.　　They are *laughing*.

- **Pronoun** A pronoun takes the place of a noun.

  Dorota bought a new car. *She* bought *it* last week.

  John likes Mary, but *she* doesn't like *him*.

- **Punctuation** The use of specific marks, such as commas and periods, to make ideas within writing clear.

- **Question Mark** ?

- **Regular Verb** A regular verb forms its past tense with *-ed*.

  He *worked* yesterday.　We *listened* to the radio.

- **-s Form** The *-s* form is a present tense verb that ends in *-s* or *-es*.

  He *lives* in New York.　She *watches* TV a lot.

- **Sentence** A sentence is a group of words that contains a subject[1] and a verb (at least) and gives a complete thought.

  SENTENCE: She came home.

  NOT A SENTENCE: When she came home.

- **Simple Form of Verb** The simple form of the verb, also called the "base" form, has no tense; it never has an *-s, -ed,* or *-ing* ending.

  Did you *see* the movie?　　　　　　I can't *find* his phone number.

- **Singular** means "one."

  She ate a *sandwich*.　I have one *television*.

- **Subject** The subject of the sentence tells who or what the sentence is about.

  My sister bought a new car.　　　　*The car* is beautiful.

- **Subject Pronoun** We use a subject pronoun (*I, you, he, she, it, we, you,* and *they*) before a verb.

  They speak Japanese.　*We* speak Spanish.

- **Superlative Form** The superlative form of an adjective or adverb shows the number one item in a group of three or more.

  January is the *coldest* month of the year.

  You have the *best* seat in the room.

---

[1] In an imperative sentence, the subject *you* is omitted: *Sit down. Come here.*

- **Syllable** A syllable is a part of a word that has only one vowel sound. (Some words have only one syllable.)

  change (one syllable) after (af • ter = two syllables)

  look (one syllable) responsible (re • spon • si • ble = four syllables)

- **Tense** A verb has tense. Tense shows when the action of the sentence happened.

  SIMPLE PRESENT: She usually *drives* to work.

  FUTURE: She *is going to drive* tomorrow.

  PRESENT CONTINUOUS: She *is driving* now.

  SIMPLE PAST: She *drove* yesterday.

- **Verb** A verb is the action of the sentence. The verb *be* connects.

  He *runs* fast. I *speak* English. You *are* late.

- **Vowel** The following letters are vowels: *a, e, i, o, u. Y* is sometimes considered a vowel (for example, in the word *mystery*).

INDEX